A
COMPREHENSIVE PROGRAM
OF
CHURCH MUSIC

A Comprehensive Program of Church Music

FEDERAL LEE WHITTLESEY

Philadelphia
THE WESTMINSTER PRESS

To my wife, Jessie,
who has patiently counseled, criticized, and com-
panioned me during the years when the ideas
contained in this book were germinating.

F. L. W.

CONTENTS

PREFACE

Some time ago I heard Stanley High say, "Happiness comes to any man who allies himself wholeheartedly to a great cause." Church music is "a great cause," and this book was compiled primarily to help those who have allied themselves to it. This does not suggest that the path of the church musician is without disappointments. Happiness for the one who has embraced this "cause," either as a profession or as an avocation, comes from the satisfaction of working with human spirits and eternal values.

In seminars, summer schools, and choir directors' courses the same questions repeatedly arise — " What ages work best together? " " What music do you recommend? " " How do you maintain interest? " " What do I do when my pastor — ? " This book seeks to give practical help in the problems one may encounter in organizing, training, and using a multiple-choir system. It also stresses the religious educational values of church choirs and the spiritual side of the ministry of music. This book is entirely the result of experience. Every idea, method, and suggestion has been used in at least one of the four churches I have served; most of them, in more than one. It is hoped that there may be a paragraph or two of inspiration in these pages, but it aims essentially to be a what-to-do and how-to-do-it book.

7

I believe there are chapters of interest and value in this book not only for the choir director and the organist, but also for the pastor, the adult singers in the choir, the directors of Christian education, and the members of the music committee. This last group has been almost entirely neglected when writers have given their ideas on church music. I believe that a conscientious layman who is appointed to a music committee will find ideas here that will help him to help his church develop a more comprehensive program of church music. The book is so planned and organized that it may be used advantageously by seminaries and schools of music in their church music courses.

It is not expected that every idea expounded here will be of interest or value to every reader. It is believed, however, that every reader, regardless of the size or nature of the church he is serving, will find many of the ideas useful in his situation.

So this book is offered to people who are finding, or wish to find, satisfying happiness in service; men and women who are wholeheartedly striving to help others attain their " chief end." I remember as a boy studying the Shorter Catechism. Its first question is, " What is the chief end of man? " The answer of authority declares, " Man's chief end is to glorify God, and to enjoy him forever."

FEDERAL LEE WHITTLESEY

Dallas, Texas

INTRODUCTION

THE DIRECTOR OF MUSIC

INTRODUCTION: THE DIRECTOR OF MUSIC

One hymn that we sing, referring to the Bible, says:

> " Thy Word is like a deep, deep mine;
> And jewels rich and rare
> Are hidden in its mighty depths
> For every searcher there." [1]

And so it is: if we search the Scriptures, we find the answers to the questions of life; they tell the seeker how to conduct himself, how to live completely. May we be so bold as to believe that the Holy Spirit inspired human writers of many centuries ago to pen phrases that will guide the mid-twentieth-century director of church music? Many truths

> " Are hidden in its mighty depths
> For every searcher there."

BIBLICAL DESCRIPTION

So we search, and in I Sam. 16:18 we find a description of the qualities that made David the greatest sacred musician of time. These same qualities stand as the requirements for a church musician today, and they form an outline of virtues toward which we should strive.

11

"One of the young men answered, ' Behold, I have seen a son of Jesse the Bethlehemite, who is skilful in playing, a man of valor, a man of war, prudent in speech, and a man of good presence; and the Lord is with him.' "

" skilful in playing . . ."

This phrase suggests that David was technically proficient on his instrument of expression. This is the goal toward which the church musician must strive. He should aim to be the best musician that he can become. This does not mean just a few years of college or conservatory attendance, but a lifetime of diligent practice, reading, listening, research, and study. The field of church music is so vast, encompassing, as it does, much of the secular field as well as all the music intended for worship, that a lifetime of concentration is too short if one is to reach the high goal that is suggested by the phrase "skilful in playing."

" a man of valor . . ."

David was brave and courageous; he had leadership qualities. A leader is one who has attainments in a certain field over and beyond those possessed by others; thus he commands their respect and their following. He is one who has courage and confidence and can impart these qualities. He has enthusiasm, for without this nothing truly great was ever accomplished.

" a man of war . . ."

This phrase does not infer that David was always fighting, but that he had the qualities that made a good soldier. What are these qualities? Among them are physical fitness, self-discipline, coolness under tension, and a firm belief in the worth of his cause. The application of each of these to the church musician is self-evident.

" prudent in speech . . ."

This seems to suggest that David was, and we should be, careful with our words, not given to exaggeration or self-exaltation, but circumspect in all we say. We should let our speech be such as is fitting for those in the high calling of Christian service.

" a man of good presence . . ."

Starting with what nature has given him, anyone can develop good presence, wholesomeness, pleasing or agreeable qualities of behavior or conduct. Anyone can develop grace and a dignified carriage; anyone can be careful about his clothing and his personal habits.

" the Lord is with him "

One may have a good measure of all the other characteristics that distinguished David, but if he fails in this final one his ministry of music will fail. It was said of David that the Lord was with him; that is, he was sincere, he was spiritual. Can that be said of us?

Let us examine ourselves in the searching light of this ancient description of the psalmist and see how nearly we meet the Scriptural requirements for one whom God can use to minister to his people through music.

The music in a church mirrors its director. A musically enlightened and spiritually sensitive worshiper can tell much about the musical, religious, and educational training of the music director by attending services in which the choir sings. Indeed, the director's philosophy of life and religion is reflected in the singing and conduct of his choirs. The selection of music and the way it is rendered will speak of his musical training. A sincere religious tone shows his own devout nature. An educated director will not tolerate slovenly diction by his choristers. A series of choirs that sing artistically, spiritually, and intelligently; that evidence a conduct becoming a group leading in worship; and that genuinely minister to the communicants, does not just happen. Such choirs are the " lengthened shadow " of the director.

QUALIFICATIONS

What qualifications does the church have a right to expect in its director of music? What attributes should the aspirant to this musical priesthood possess?

He Must Be a Christian

He should lead a life known for its Christian integrity. He must be unquestionably sincere. Unfortunately, churches have at times entrusted their musical leadership to persons not possessing this first qualification. The results have made " change and decay " synonymous. This is not the only attribute the director should have, but without this all others will not be sufficient to produce anything of permanent worth.

He should be a member of the church he is serving. Experience has shown that where he is not, there is less apt to be an interest in building and maintaining a worthy program.

He Should Be a Trained Musician

Churches are realizing that good musicianship is a highly desirable attribute of a choir leader. But what is good musicianship, and when may a person be considered to possess it? A good musician will have adequate performing technique on some instrument or in voice; he will have studied the theory of music; he will have a working knowledge of musical history and musical literature. Because there are always challenging fields into which he has not delved, a musician worthy of the name never ceases to study. A person without a sound musical judgment may perpetrate many a tonal monstrosity in the name of worship music. For instance, the writer once heard Handel's " Hallelujah Chorus " sung unaccompanied and in the style of a glee.

He Should Be Specifically Trained in the Music of the Church

Because one has had a good general musical training, it does not follow that he is equipped to lead in the music of the church. A special preparation is highly desirable. He should study the history of church music. He should study liturgies and the music used in them. He should be versed in the extensive repertoire of sacred music. He should learn how music may be used as a medium of religious expression and how, through it, he may minister to the spiritual needs of a congregation. Until comparatively recently, opportunity for specialized study of this kind was limited. Now, however, there is little excuse for one who desires to do church work to be untrained. Many colleges and conservatories have departments of church music. In several parts of the country, short, concentrated summer courses for church musicians are conducted by authorities in this field. Opportunities to become skilled in the music of the church are abundant.

He Should Be Able to Train Voices

Because one is a good organist, it does not necessarily follow that he can train voices. Even if one can sing well, it does not inevitably ensue that it is safe to put him in charge of a choir. The church should see to it that the one engaged to lead a choral program has been schooled in training voices.

Some voice teachers will not let their students sing in church choirs. If choirs are directed by people with little or no understanding of the voice, harm may be done, harm that a teacher cannot overcome in lessons. Choir singing is excellent practice for singers if the director knows voice production.

He Should Have a Good General Education

He must meet and should deserve the respect of all classes of people. A good general education will help him do this. It is particularly necessary for him to use good English. He also must understand correct accents and pronunciations, not only because of his own speech, but because with this understanding he has a valuable aid in voice training.

He Should Have a Personality That Will Command Attention

There is a decided difference between commanding and demanding attention. The one who commands attention by the power of his magnetism has no disciplinary problem. The one who is constantly demanding attention is merely showing the weakness of his own nature. He should ever strive to enrich his personality that he may better lead his singers in service to others.

The Director Must Have Tact

The person who lacks this important virtue, tact, will have a difficult time as a choral director. What oil is to machinery, tact is to dealing with people. When a clash of personalities or ideas occurs, it is tact that keeps things moving smoothly when heat and friction might otherwise arise. It is such a temptation for a director to be cleverly sarcastic when some offensive person has spoken out of turn. This must be avoided, for, boomeranglike, it always reflects on the director.

The director should be approachable to his singers but not too intimate with them. He should possess a sense of humor and know just how and when to use it. He must be a father to some, a shepherd to others, and a practical psychologist in handling all.

The Director Should Be a Student of Public Worship

The trend is toward enriching the worship services. Everywhere may be found an increasing amount of ritual, even among the so-called nonliturgical churches. The extemporaneous service so prevalent a few decades ago has largely given way to a more carefully planned, psychologically correct service. The director must study this and be able to fit his music into it.

The Director Should Be an Indefatigable Worker

A forty-hour week is not for the choir director. An energetic leader will find he needs many hours for all that must be done. There may be private voice lessons to be given to choir members. This may be the best method of getting and holding members for the adult choir. There are calls to be made. The director should make a call at the home of each of his choristers once a year. Especially with the child chorister is this important. The co-operation of the parents is essential in maintaining the children's choirs; a call in the home may provide the necessary aid. There are classes in musicianship to be taught. Several rehearsals must be prepared and directed each week. There are hours of study, planning, and conferences, besides practice on his own instrument or vocalizing if he is a singer.

Of course, all directors of church music are not in a position where they can give full time to their church. Meager church salaries often make it necessary to have outside remuneration. But even when this is the case, the director must be willing to put in many hours of teaching and directing beyond " the call of duty." The success of a church music program is generally in direct proportion to the amount of time the leader puts into it. Yearly, more churches are realizing this and are becoming willing to pay for a competent, full-time director of music.

The Director Should Be an Inspiration to Those Under Him

He should be an inspiration to them mentally, physically, vocally, artistically, and spiritually. The adage, " Water will rise no higher than its source," applies here. Let a choir once feel that the director has become stagnant — that he has ceased to grow — and its inspiration is gone. A leader must stay ahead to lead; he must himself be inspired to inspire.

If the church has a right to expect all these qualities in its director of music, hasn't the director the right to expect some things from the church? Certainly he has. He should have freedom in handling all matters pertaining to the choir. This will include the selection of singers without pressure from the pastor or the music committee. He should have complete say about the music to be used. If the director has the aforementioned qualifications, he can be trusted. Then too the director is entitled to adequate compensation. Just what that is depends on the size of the church and the amount of time the director gives, his experience, and other considerations.

SUCCESSFUL LEADERSHIP

During World War II an admiral said that it took " three ships to win a battle at sea — craftsmanship, seamanship, marksmanship." It takes these same three ships to be a success as a leader in church music.

Craftsmanship

A good craftsman is one who knows all the tools of a trade and knows how to use them. The director of music should be a master of his craft.

Seamanship

A ship is said to be " seaworthy " when it is well constructed and will ride the waves. Then it is worthy to be trusted. The director must prove himself worthy to be trusted with this important activity of the church — its music. A sailor is said to have seamanship when he can handle the ship and when he knows the tides, currents, and winds and can guide the ship to avoid the hazards. The analogy to the director is obvious.

Marksmanship

The ship's gunners must be able to hit the mark. What is the mark or the general goal at which the music director is aiming? It is to develop good choirs for the enriching of public worship and the bringing of spiritual values into the life of each singer.

PART ONE

CHOIRS

THE MULTIPLE CHOIR SYSTEM

The Christian church, like no other organization on earth,
is concerned with human beings from youngest childhood
through old age. It endeavors to enrich life by bringing
the individual into a close relationship with his Creator
through worship, and by guiding him into paths of Christian fellowship and service. Music is one ready means of
assisting the church in this high purpose. Music has great
potential as a cultural medium, as a social medium, and
as an entertaining medium. However, the church's chief
use of it is none of these; it is to ennoble life and character.

If music is to be used in ministering to this end, it should
be music by and for all the people. This conception of
music's use in the church leads to choirs for different ages,
functioning for the spiritual development of the individual singer and as aids in corporate worship. This logically
calls for a series of choirs, graded according to age and
ability, which will give to all who wish to do so an opportunity to participate.

The extent of the graded choir plan in any given church
is dependent upon many conditions. The size of the church
and church school must be considered. Eight to ten per
cent of the combined membership are potential partici-

pants in the choir system. That is, many people have interest and ability, and if approached convincingly will
take their place in some phase of the music program. The
distance the people live from the church will have a bear-
ing. A downtown church will have difficulty with youth
choirs; a community church has an advantage. The active
musical interests of the parish as a whole will be an indication of what response may be expected. The amount of
time the director can give will influence the number of
choirs attempted. Much better to do a thorough job of a
few choirs than a superficial job with many. The amount
of volunteer lay help available has a relationship. The
director cannot " go it alone." He must have sufficient and
efficient help to organize, train, and carry on the activities
of a multiple-choir system. The actual amount of co-
operation the pastor and the religious education department will give also will guide the director of music in
determining the number of choirs he can develop and use
effectively.

The graded choir plan must fit the church; the church
ought not to be asked to fit the director's preconceived
plan. Because a certain choir plan works in one church
under particular conditions, it does not mean that it will
work in another. The wise director will build slowly and
firmly, adding choirs as there is a need. He will aim toward
the goal of giving an opportunity for all to have a part in
the musical expression of worship.

THE PURPOSES OF CHOIRS FOR CHILDREN
AND JUNIOR HIGHS

Many directors do not have a clear insight as to why
choirs for children and junior high young people are im-

portant and what can be accomplished by organizing and training them. Before we go into a discussion of the individual choirs of a graded choir system, it may be well to consider the general subject of these younger choirs. There are many definite things that may be achieved with and through choirs of children.

Choirs Train for Work in the Church

Through choirs we can help children and young people to find their places in the life and work of the church. Churches are in the long run built from the children up. The church school is chiefly for them, but the worship service, which is the central act of the life of the church, often makes little provision for children.

One excellent way to help youngsters feel that the worship service is for them as well as for adults is to have children's choirs take a regular and active part in the worship. The accusation is sometimes made that children's choirs detract from the worship service because of poor singing and unbecoming deportment. This need not be true. A choir of children can be taught to sing beautifully, to conduct itself with decorum, and to add worship values to the service. Whether this is done or not seems to be wholly up to the director. However, if the children receive something of definite spiritual value from participation, that is of more importance than that the adults be pleased. The churchgoing habit has been formed in older folks, but in youth it is in the process of cultivation. It is important to keep youth coming to church regularly. *Frequent appearance of the children's choir fosters a church-attending habit.* The actual frequency of choirs' appearances should, of course, vary with the age groups involved.

Choirs Teach Reverence and Worship

In the choir we have an ideal situation in which to teach reverence and worship. This is something that should be taught to all adults and children if we expect them ever to enter into the deeper experiences of communion with God. Generally no time or place is provided to teach youth or adults how to worship, what worship is, the meaning of the different parts of the worship service, or what their attitude toward worship should be.

In music appreciation classes we are taught that a trio — an inspired composer, an imaginative performer, and an intelligent listener — is necessary for the full import of music. Similarly, for the complete effectiveness of a worship service a trio is required. Worthy, inspired materials must be used, that is, liturgies, hymns, anthems, prayers, and such. The leaders — minister, musical director, and singers — must be thoroughly trained, sincere, and spiritually minded. To these must be added an enlightened, religiously sensitive, and responsive congregation. To complete the worship trio, the people should know something of music and how to listen to it; they should know the historical and religious significance of the various parts of the worship service; they should know how mentally and spiritually to approach the worship of Almighty God.

The director cannot hope to teach all this to the congregation; in fact, it is not his responsibility to do so. He will, however, if he is wise, try to instill into the minds of his choristers of all ages how they should prepare for worship. Many of these so instructed will be in the congregation in later years. (He must not expect, nor should he want, all who come into a choir system to remain in it over too long a period of years.) These will form the leaven which will permeate the whole and bring an unfeigned adoration of the Supreme Being. *Enrich the lives of your choristers by teaching them how to worship.*

Choirs Teach Correct Habits of Singing

In younger choirs correct habits of singing can be taught. It is much easier to instill right singing habits in children than to overcome faulty ones in adults. One aspect of singing is a muscle development. This can best be taught while the muscles are pliable, that is, during childhood. *Establish good singing habits in children's voices, and you will be assured of beauty in adult voices.*

Choirs Teach Fundamentals of Music

Some purely musical subjects should be taught. At least the elements of notation, rhythmic study, and ear training can be instilled into the minds of choir children. Most children get the beginning of a musical training in the public schools, and some of them have private music instruction. The wise director will add to this instruction and tie it up to his own music by supplemental training. Children learn readily by rote, but this does not train sight readers. What can be done along this line depends on the amount of time the director has the children each week. If more than one rehearsal is held with each choir each week, real progress can be made. Keep the far perspective of what you are to do with the children. Help them to learn to read music. *Prepare children for a lifetime of music in the church.*

Choirs Teach the Great, Lasting Hymns of the Church

The procedure at this point should be very carefully planned. The number of hymns that the average congregation knows and can sing well is surprisingly small. This is not the congregation's fault but that of its leadership; its members should have been taught a larger hymn repertoire while they were young. Teach the children's choirs at least a few of the abiding hymns each year. You will find that you cannot do justice to many in a choir season. Ask your pastor's help in selecting the most worth-while new hymns to teach. His interest and co-operation will lead him to choose these same hymns for the worship services. Teach the children about the authors or sources, the composers, the tune names, the various meters. Explain the use to which the hymns might be put in a worship service. It is more important that the children be learning the hymns of faith than that they learn anthems to sing in public. Of course, they must do that also. *Do not fail to teach your choristers the church's heritage of song.*

Choirs Develop Singers for Future Choirs

Children's choirs develop singers for fine adult choirs of later years and for a singing congregation. The church that has a graded choir system in operation has a distinct advantage. It is training its own singers " in the way they should go " and providing a constant stream of talent eager for membership in the next older choir. It takes only a few years for the value of a graded choir system to be felt in the adult choir. *The farseeing director will build toward the future by training the children now.*

Choirs Provide a Large Body of Singers for Festival Occasions

There are several events in the church year that call strongly for numbers of singers. A Thanksgiving or Harvest Home service, an Easter service, a church anniversary, and Christmas all seem to be more impressive when several choirs join in leading the congregation in its paeans. Children's choirs participating in these events are particularly impressive. A carefully executed processional of several choirs returns a bit of needed pageantry to an institution made barren of much of its early beauty by Puritanic restrictions. *Combined choirs can make such a service a festival.*

Choirs Are an Evangelizing Agent

One test of a children's and youth choir program is how many join the church as a result of it — not children alone, but parents too. The children will be reached largely through the church school; the parents, largely through the children. The director should make every effort to get the co-operation of the parents in regard to the choirs and to arouse interest in the full church program. (A note to the finance committee: many churches feel that a well-organized graded choir system pays its way by the contributing members it brings into the church.) *Seek to bring the whole family into the church life.*

Choirs Help Mold Lives for Christ

The director can find joy as he molds lives for Christ. If the director has a genuine love of children and a love of the church, it is easy and satisfying to bring them together. Children are very impressionable. The director can make an imprint upon them that may be seen throughout their lives. It is a great trust that is put in his hands, and if he discharges it faithfully, it returns as a great delight.

It would be difficult to overemphasize the value of painstaking and persistent effort in behalf of the children's and youth choirs. The director's joy will increase as he sees children developing under his guidance. The pastor's joy will increase as he finds the growing interest of the young people in the church. The church fathers' joy will increase as they find new families becoming interested in the whole church program.

THE YOUNGEST CHOIR

What ages are best to use for various children's choirs? There can be no answer to this question that will be an unfailing guide for every church.

Among the conditions that will affect an answer are: the number of children in the various church school departments and therefore potentially available; whether or not the children's choirs are to be part of a graded choir program with a graduation or promotion conducted from one choir to another; the amount of time the director can give to developing the choirs.

The age groupings for the choristers should be those which will make for maximum efficiency in rehearsal and minimum discipline problems, get the best singing from the child, and do the most for the child's development — musically, physically, and spiritually.

ORGANIZATION

The ages from five or six to eight years old will be found acceptable for the youngest choir in a graded choir plan. At this age they are being taught the beginnings of work and study in the public school. The church music director, taking his cue from the school, may start his church music training with this age also.

If the church is a downtown church in a large city, it probably will be judged unfeasible to have a choir of this age. The problem of regularity of attendance will be insurmountable. If, however, yours is a church in a residential district, there will be enough parents who will make the effort to bring children to rehearsals regularly to warrant organizing a carol choir, or whatever you wish to call it.

This choir should be open to all children of the specified ages, regardless of the individual's vocal ability. It is wise, however, for the director to hear each child sing before accepting him. In this way the director knows what he has to work with, and it will show him which ones need special guidance. Even a perfunctory tryout will give the children and the parents the feeling that the child has been selected.

RECRUITING

Recruiting this age will not be a difficult problem. Letters to the parents of church school members will generally produce results. The parents must be assured that the time used to bring the child to rehearsals will be compensated for in his musical and spiritual development. The choir must not be just another hour-consuming group activity. Talks to the parents in groups (as to a " Home Builders " class) or individually (by phone or personal call) will reinforce the message of the letter.

Prospects for this choir and for all choirs may be obtained from the pastoral calls on the parish. The director should always be alert for recruits from the new families that join the church or church school.

What and How to Teach '

This age is not too early to begin teaching the importance of regularity, punctuality, and discipline. You will have to train many parents in regularity and punctuality too. The young director may be surprised to find that many of the important virtues of human behavior are not too well instilled in young America by the training received at home.

At the age when the child is starting his formal school education, it is not too early for him to start choir education also. Many of the basic elements that will make for an enriched life through music and the church can begin to be developed in the child at five, six, and seven years. Some of these are: good singing, by insisting on correct posture, breathing, ease of singing, and correct pronunciation; the beginning of identifying musical symbols — notes, rests, measures; respect for appointed authority as invested in the director; respect for the church and its music; reverence and some of the meanings of worship.

Rehearsals should start on time, with some definite signal: maybe the ringing of a bell, or a chord on the piano, or the striking of a tuning bar. The starting signal means no more talking and may aptly be followed with a quieting prayer. The rehearsal should be started with an admonition for and illustration of good posture and by tone matching and sustaining. I find the A tuning bar interests the children, and I have them tune their voices to it first. Then I take other tones for matching: up and down a short " ladder " or " elevator " (three tones) ; a medium " ladder " (five tones) ; and the long " stepladder " (scales) . In teaching children, it is best to make games; action songs or active vocalizations interest them. The rehearsals must be fun as well as instructive.[2]

In patterning for your children, it is important that they hear the pitch clearly and accurately given, without vibrato, and that the pronunciation, inflection, and mood be correct. It may be, if the director is a woman, that the director can do it effectively; in lieu of that, a young lady should be found whose voice meets the requirements. She should sit in the choir regularly (at least in rehearsals, and it may be necessary at performances also) and sing exactly as the director wants the children to sing. A violin played well in tune and without vibrato is a possible substitute for the above arrangement. A piano or organ for patterning is not too good. Keep in mind that children are natural imitators, and learn primarily by following an example and by repetition. This age will not be able to read words rapidly. Words as well as music must be taught by rote. Remember, the children will imitate the pronunciation, inflection, and facial expression of the one who teaches them.

The words and music the director expects this choir to sing must be simple and direct. Words that deal with God in nature, a God of love, or Jesus as a babe will probably be best understood by the children. The music should be of restricted compass, rarely more than a ninth or tenth. This choir should seldom be asked to sing above the E on the treble staff. The music for this choir should be chiefly diatonic.

The repertoire should consist of a few simple hymns, a few songs that might be used in services, and many interesting teaching songs. In this last category, one book is indispensable for me: it is *Our First Music*.[3] This book has many numbers both sacred and secular from which the children will profit and with which they will have fun.

Some have to be adapted or transposed lower, I feel, but the book's 362 pages will provide a treasure house of workable music for the very young choir.

INTERPRETING THE LOVE OF GOD

The children will respond to the director who evidences a love for them. Their conception of a God of love is largely defined by the personalities and characters of their parents and church teachers. The choir director interprets God to the choristers more than the pastor does. Most of the children, not coming to the worship service regularly, do not have much contact with the pastor. The director must love his children and show it. If he does, he will have no disciplinary problem, for the children will love and respect their director too.

PUBLIC APPEARANCE

The primary purpose of this choir is the religious training of the child through a musical medium. This choir should not appear in public often; twice a year is sufficient. It may properly sing in a Christmas program and again on Children's Day. It may be desirable to have the entire choir system appear on other occasions, but at such times these children should be expected only to add interest and picturesqueness.

3

THE JUNIOR CHOIR

When properly organized and trained, the junior choir can be the source of much benefit to the chorister and to the church.

The title " junior choir " is used in various churches to indicate various ages. For the purpose of this chapter the name will mean both boys and girls of eight, nine, ten, and eleven years of age.

RECRUITING

Prospects for this choir will come from several sources. Some children will be promoted each year from the youngest choir. Others will come from the church school. To bring these in, announcement may be made in the department that has this junior-choir age, or letters may be sent to the children and parents whose names appear in the church school files. The pastor and director of education will give you names of children to contact. Interested choristers, like satisfied customers, bring others.

Tryout

The director should privately hear each applicant sing. A simple test is all that is necessary. This so-called " tryout " is not to eliminate any child, but to show the director what he has to work with and where his greatest efforts must be put. The director can determine the child's ability to " carry a tune " by having him sing a song that he knows; " America " will suffice. Does he have a " musical ear " ? The applicant should be checked on his ability to reproduce, by his own voice, tones he hears from the piano. This can be done by the director's playing two or three note patterns and requesting the child to imitate the tones he hears. The child is not expected to be able to read music. If the candidate can sing the melody of " America " and can accurately imitate the tones he hears, you have all that is necessary from the vocal standpoint as a prerequisite for a junior chorister. If the child is physically and mentally alert, he will make a better singer than a passive child; he will be harder to keep interested, but will be more engaging too.

Monotones

If a child applies who seems to be a "monotone," be not too hasty in your judgment of him. Many children who appear not to be able to modulate their voices need only a little coaching and encouraging before they will sense how to produce tone. If the child does not learn in early youth to make variations in pitch, he probably never will. There are people who are tone-deaf, but they are extremely rare. The director should encourage him and test him often to see if tonal consciousness is being awakened in him. Patience and persistence will help many so-called " monotones " to " find " their voices.

SIZE OF CHOIR

The number of children who may be accepted for this choir will be determined by several things. There must not be more in a choir than can comfortably be handled in the choir loft. Do not take more in the choir than the number of vestments available. You must guide the singing of the choristers individually as well as collectively, so too large a choir is not advisable. Thirty seems to be a satisfactory number to handle, as well as being a sufficient number to give good tone work. If a large number of children desire membership, duplicate choirs are recommended. They may sing together in public if space and vestments permit, but they should rehearse separately. Plan your choir so as to have a waiting list. If there are those eager for membership who cannot get in because the choir roster is complete, the choristers will be much more diligent. This works as well with adults as with children.

What and How to Teach

Voice training with a junior choir must be approached on a simple, easily understood, and vocally correct method. Such an approach may be outlined as follows:

Sit or Stand Erect

Only erect posture while singing must be tolerated. Good tone can never come from a slouching or sluggish body. Natural, correct breathing, an essential for good tone, will result if the chorister learns how to sit upright. If the child does not seem able to assume this position, balance a book on his head and have him raise it as high as possible. This will straighten the spine, lift the sternum, bring the side ribs out, and allow a full and correct inhalation and exhalation of air. Make a game of assuming and maintaining correct posture. Make a mark on the choir-room blackboard whenever a chorister slumps. Of course the choristers have a right to make a similar mark on the board when the director slumps.

Teach the melody of the well-known round " Frère Jacques," with the words:

" Perfect posture, perfect posture,
   Do not slump, do not slump.
 You must grow up handsome, you must grow up handsome,
   Hide that hump, hide that hump."

— Anonymous

This song can be sung with motions; so used, it will particularly interest the children and is good activity for them. On singing the first and third lines they must sit very erect; on line two they slide down in the chairs; on line four they bend over. Attempting this song as a round with eight-, nine-, and ten-year-olds will be found unsuccessful, but it may be done with older children.

The director should never conduct while any chorister is inattentive or in poor posture. Of course brief moments of relaxation between songs are necessary.

Sing Easily

Most children sing too loudly. They should be given songs that will encourage ease of singing. It is wise to use a gentle tone of voice when speaking or singing to children. Sweetness and lightness are the qualities to be sought in the junior choir's singing.

Sing Naturally

Children seem prone to imitate the bad rather than the good traits in the singing of their elders. When the juniors see a pseudovocalist pucker his lips in a hooting position while uttering an $\bar{oo}$ vowel, or draw the corners of his mouth back in a grin for $\bar{e}$, or emit a starry gape while endeavoring to sing an *ah,* they instinctively copy. The children must be taught to sing as nature intended, that is, with a simple, unaffected production and pronunciation. Simple vocalizing is beneficial if the above three principles are maintained. It is wise to do early vocalizing with the vowel sound of $\bar{oo}$ (as in " who "), gradually working into others. All vowels must be colored by the quality of this vowel $\bar{oo}$. It is beneficial to take melodic passages from songs being studied and to use them as vocalises. They may be transposed up and down within the comfortable range of the voices.

This is obviously not intended as a thorough course in child voice training. Many choirs should be listened to, many choirmasters' methods studied, many books by successful directors read before one attempts to train that most delicate musical instrument, the child's voice.

Musicianship and Ear Training

Some forms of musicianship training should be started with this choir. The primary note values can be taught. The children can become familiar with whole, half, and quarter notes and rests and can know their related values. The children will gain much from learning how to beat time at least for triple and quadruple measure. They can all learn to make the hand go down-right-up for triple measure and down-left-right-up for quadruple. This may be tied up to note values as well as to the director's hand motions while conducting a hymn or anthem. The children should be drilled to hear accurately, and to reproduce with their voices accurately, tones played on a well-tuned piano or played by a good violinist. Simple two- or three-note patterns, chiefly within a major scale, may first be used. Later, longer exercises and more unrelated tones may be attempted. Make a game of it. Divide up the choir; see which side is the more accurate. Tricky intervals from songs being learned may be studied advantageously in this way.

Voice and musicianship training must be done regularly if they are to be of value; they must be presented interestingly if the children are going to enjoy them and profit by them. Children respond much more readily to an exercise that seems like a spontaneous game than they do to routine practice. Make the exercise a test of skill rather than an imposed task.

Hymns and anthems must be taught to the juniors primarily by rote. The piano, a voice, or a violin may be used as a teaching medium. If the piano is used, the following method is suggested: The children may be asked to close their eyes while listening to the melody for a time or two; then they may be asked questions about the melody: " What does it make you think of? Does it laugh with joy or sound like a prayer? Is it happy or sad? What kind of words should be used with that melody? " Then the words may be read to them. Extreme care should be taken to use the correct pronunciation and inflection in the reading. If the music is in simple meter and form, as it should be for this choir, the children may beat time for a few playings. Now come back to the words, explain them, paraphrase them. Let the children follow them as the music is played again. They are now ready to sing the song for the first time. If their minds have been thus prepared, they will do surprisingly well on the first attempt. If a voice is used as a pattern, the singer must be very carefully coached for tone quality, pronunciation, and expression. Remember that children are mimics. If the director has a good violinist available, it will be helpful to use him to pattern for the children. The tone of the children should more nearly reproduce the violin tone than that of any other instrument.

Interpreting hymns and anthems will offer no great problem if the words are readily understood by the children. If the words appeal to their imaginations, or if the explanation and illustration can be made to appeal, this will sufficiently color their singing. This choir, learning its music chiefly by rote, will always sing from memory in public.

Children must be active. The wise director, realizing this, will plan for and control the activity of his choir. He is obliged to consider both physical and mental activity. In the rehearsal, and also in the service, provision must be made for this childhood energy.

The Rehearsal

The rehearsal should give occasion for the chorister to do many different things. Remember that the concentration span of a child of junior choir age, even under the most favorable conditions, is very brief. The physical-stillness span is only slightly longer.

The rehearsal should begin on time. A chord may be played which the children know means attention. The director may then open rehearsal with a quieting prayer.

Some of the activities that may be used in the rehearsal procedure might be as follows: vocalizing with attention to the fundamentals of singing; ear training; note-value study; time beating for rhythm and accent, the accompanist playing a hymn the children are learning; singing a simple round or action song; processional practice around the room; reading and discussing the words of a hymn or anthem; standing to review a song; working on new material; standing for physical exercise combined with a little vocalizing; back to the new song and, making a game of it, seeing which row of the choir knows it best; explaining the significance of some part of the worship service, for example, the prelude, Doxology, or offertory; telling of an activity of another choir of the system; closing with a short religious ritual or at least a prayer.

It is not suggested that all the above be done at any one rehearsal. However, all this and much more will be covered at various rehearsals by the inventive director who understands the psychology of handling and interesting children.

Singing in Worship Service

In planning the church service when the children sing, the leaders must take into consideration the childhood characteristic of activity. A child usually cannot sit still very long at a time, so it is wise to have the junior choir seated where it will not be too well seen by the congregation. The juniors should sing in the early part of a service. They should not be expected to sit through a half-hour sermon intended for adults. It may be best to have them leave soon after they have sung and go to a junior church.

The junior choir will sing in public only a few times in the season: at a choir dedication service in the fall, at a Christmas service, once or twice in a regular service with another choir, possibly at an Easter service, and at a Children's Day service. The function of this choir is not so much to prepare anthems for public services as it is to help create Christian character through religious music.

RECOGNITION OF PROGRESS

Every phase of the work of a choir should be systematically carried out. Records of attendance, punctuality, vocal progress, co-operation, and so on, should be carefully kept.

Particularly good records should be acknowledged with some kind of recognition. It may seem that ideally we should strive for the joy of serving a worthy cause; practically, some award for the striving has a clear appeal. Most successful choir directors use some award system. Equal awards should be presented to all who meet a prescribed standard.

THE ELEVEN-YEAR-OLD

Though the preceding is intended to be the choir for the children up to junior high school, it may be well to consider some of the problems and possibilities of the eleven-year-old.

The span of eight through eleven is a wide one when consideration is given to the increased physical development and mental quickening of the last year. The eleven-year-old girl is capable of much better work than the eight- or nine-year-old. Her voice is better, her reading is much faster, her worship-leadership potentials are greater. She is apt to feel that the junior choir has nothing for her, that it isn't worth the effort. It often happens that she is engrossed in some interesting girls' club activity and drops out of choir. The director must use his best child psychology to hold the girl of this age.

If the junior choir is relatively small, the eleven-year-old girl may be necessary for the good work of the choir. If so, these girls should be given special responsibilities such as checking on attendance, having the room in order, having music ready. If the choir is big enough without them, it may be best to have a special choir for this age. This is the age of "gang consciousness," of a desire to "belong." It should not be too difficult to get a group of ten to twenty or more girls of this age to band together and form a special choir. They should be challenged with really important responsibilities. It may be necessary to treat them like a club with social as well as musical activities. It is important to hold this group for the church and for the choir system.

Let us consider the eleven-year-old boy. He probably is not too eager to sit beside the girls. He is a little slower at learning the music, but once he gets it he can sing with a good firm tone. He considers eight- and nine-year-olds as babies. He would rather be with a bunch of boys fishing or playing football. If the director had to use his best skill with girls this age, what superingenuity can he use with the boys! A director will be quite largely judged by how he handles boys and men. How many can he attract to the choirs and to the church? His choir system will stand or fall at this point. It behooves him to study his boys, to gain their good will and interest individually, and to know where he can place them for the best advantage of the boy and the choir.

Although a choir system is set up on an age basis, an individual may work better when he is with an older or younger group. I have found that the eleven-year-old boy is stimulated for his best work when he is with older boys. Thus I take this age boy into the boy choir which is normally a junior high choir.

THE CHOIR BOOK

STIMULATING INTEREST

One device that has been found to be invaluable in stimulating the interest of all young choristers is the choir book. It gives them tangible material to show about their choir; it gives them the feeling that there is something new each week as they receive new pages; it makes possible all kinds of instruction and information; it gives them a little " homework "; and it allows parents to follow the activities and progress of the chorister.

At a rehearsal early in the season each chorister is given a booklet consisting of a loose-leaf cover with some mimeographed sheets. The cover should be of a different color for each choir. The cost of the book is borne by the church. The first sheet may be an inspirational page with a picture of Jesus or of the church. Or better yet, there may be a place for such a picture which the chorister must find and paste in. A second page may be a title page with the name of the church, choir, and chorister to be filled in by the child.

ATTENDANCE RECORDS

The next page in the choir book can well be an attendance record page. This page can give the information as to what is expected in attendance, excuses, and calling the director about absences. It should also have a square for each rehearsal and service. When the child brings the book to rehearsal he presents it to the secretary, who checks it for attendance (or tardiness), for previous excused or unexcused absence, and for the bringing of his choir book. The secretary checks both the choir book and the director's roll book. At the end of the month a seal is given for a perfect attendance record.

INSTRUCTION SHEETS

If an award system is in use, it is well to have a page or two explaining this to the chorister and the parents. A pledge for the chorister and the parents to sign can be put on another page. It is recommended that rehearsals open and close with prayer; a page or two of prayers or litanies appropriate for such use can be included. Asking the children to write their own choir prayer is helpful.

A week before each singing in public, a page of instruction about the time, place of meeting, vestments, and so forth, should be given to the children for their choir books. This gives the chorister and the parents the information they will need.

HYMN AND ANTHEM STUDY

A part of the choir's activity will be directed toward learning the timeless hymns of the church. Pages for the choir book can be prepared that will aid in this. Such pages will include information about the composer, author, or source; the tune name; the meter; the mood of the hymn; and how to use it in a service of worship. If the

" Hymn of the Month " plan is followed, choir book pages can assist in promoting it.

Of course, separate octavo anthems will be purchased and used by the children's choir, but even then choir book pages can be prepared that will help the study and understanding of the anthem. These pages can give pertinent information about the author or composer, explain the musical form of the anthem, single out unusual words for definition, call attention to correct pronunciations, and in many ways help in the teaching and understanding of the anthem.

MUSICIANSHIP STUDY

The director will want to improve the musicianship of the choristers. Choir book pages form a ready tool. Notes and rests, rhythms, keys, signatures, marks of expression, intervals, and other phases of musical notation can be taught through carefully developed pages.

The writer has often made it a practice to omit the measure bars when he writes off music for the choir book. The children have to put them in. When this or any " homework " is correctly done a seal is put on the page.

USING THE CHOIR BOOK FOR RELIGIOUS EDUCATION PURPOSES

The rehearsal period should contain some elements of religious education. Most children do not have much weekday religious training. The true minister of music will want to make the rehearsal hours count toward the enrichment of life and the development of Christian character. This can and should be done in complete co-operation with the director of Christian education and the pastor. The study in the choir should supplement and complement the instruction in the corresponding age class in the church school.

For many years the writer has had some special project each season with his choristers. It is some study plan that can be a part, though often brief, of each rehearsal. Each season some subject is chosen for study that is akin to the choir's main function but not directly related to the singing of anthems. An effort is made to pick subjects that probably will not be covered in the church school curriculum but that are associated with that instruction. Mimeographed choir book pages have been a great help in the development and teaching of the special projects.

The following paragraphs will give some suggestions as to subjects that have been used.

Symbolism

Every church has some symbolism built into it. Acquainting the children with the symbols and their interpretation will enrich young lives and make worship more meaningful. Christian symbols came into being to teach, to remind, and to beautify. Choir book pages can be developed that will trace the use of symbols from the first reference (Gen. 9:13–16), through Jesus' use in his teachings, parables, and the sacraments he instituted, to the early Christians' drawings in the catacombs, and contemporary treatment.

For a list of books that will give background information for this study, see the bibliography at the end of this chapter.

Interfaith Study

How many of the children in the choirs — or parents, for that matter — have ever seen a Torah, heard a shophar, eaten matzo, or been in a synagogue? Then how can they comprehend the Old Testament, feel a kinship with Jesus' early training, or understand their Jewish neighbors? A study of the Jewish faith with its basic manifestations will lead to understanding; understanding will lead to tolerance and brotherhood.

Again, how many of the choristers understand their Catholic friends when they speak of saying a rosary, going to confession, being confirmed, or praying before the stations of the cross? How many have visited a Catholic church? A study of this faith with its cardinal beliefs will bring an understanding. The children will learn a little of what their Catholic friends believe and will gain a respect for their faith. The director should point out the areas of beliefs similar to ours, the areas of difference, and why we believe as we do. He should also point out

> " How good it is,
>   How beautiful it is
>   For brethren to live together in unity " [4]

(Copyright, 1932, by M. Witmark & Sons. Used by permission.)

and mutual understanding though they do not hold the same views. And " how good it is " that we live in a country where this is possible!

Many choir book pages can be developed to assist in this

brotherhood study. Field trips to a Jewish synagogue or
temple and to a Catholic church where the rabbi and priest
can talk to the children will be most helpful. Books and
pamphlets that will help the director prepare for this
study are listed at the end of the chapter.

Things We See and Hear in Church

One season my children's choirs made a study of things
we see and hear in church that help us to worship God.
Some of the points could have been treated under symbolism another year. Among the items discussed were:

What is worship?

Why can we best worship God in church? This led to
the answer that became the subject for the whole year's
project.

The message of the chimes.

The modified Gothic style of the church with its nave,
transepts, chancel, baptismal font, altar, carvings, and
arches.

The light-shades which reminded us of an ancient tower.
This in turn suggested the hymn " A Mighty Fortress Is
Our God " and Ps. 46.

The Gloria Patri, its history and use.

The Doxology, its origin, and why we sing it.

The meaning of vestments.

The message of flowers.

The open Bible.

Many other things could have been added to this list
for explanation if time with the choirs had permitted.

Mimeographed pages of art work and questions to be
answered by the children kept this study before them week
after week.

Great Christians

A consideration of the lives of a few renowned Christians can well form the special study for choirs for several years. If only those connected with music were chosen, this list would include Saint Francis, Martin Luther, John Wesley, Albert Schweitzer, and possibly others. Good books are available on each of these men, and these will help the director to plan a course for the children. Some are listed in the bibliography at the end of this chapter. From some of these books written for children, like *Song of St. Francis* and *Martin Luther,* I have read a chapter at each rehearsal, as the choristers were learning songs they had written. Choir book pages of questions and pictures of these men can be created to accompany the stories.

Another approach to this study of great men who influenced or were influenced by church music is to single out composers who began as choirboys. This can include Bach, Haydn, Schubert, and many others.

Music in the Bible

The many references to music, musical instruments, songs, and singers that are found in the Bible form an interesting study for young choristers. The director will need to do considerable research in preparing this, but that will be good for him also.

There are over one hundred and fifty passages in the Old Testament that refer to musical instruments. The instruments most commonly referred to are: harp, psaltery, lute, organ, pipe, trumpet, ram's-horn cornet, tabor, timbrel, and cymbals. The New Testament also has some references to these instruments.

There are two hundred and thirty-one references to " singing," " song," and " singers " in the Bible. Groups of singers (choirs) are much in evidence too.

The Psalms are not the only passages in Scripture that were sung by our religious ancestors. A study of the songs of both the Old and New Testaments will interest the children.

Church Windows

Every church has windows. They may be elaborate ecclesiastical art windows, or they may be just multicolored glass. The windows of a church can form an interesting religio-educational project.

A brief history of the art can be followed up with pictures of famous windows and choir book drawings of windows to be colored. This can be tied up to the windows the children see in their own church. The religious symbolism of color, the significance of the designs in the windows, the stories suggested by the events depicted, all can be made meaningful to the children.

REPORT OF THE YEAR'S WORK

The writer has made it a practice to call in the choir books about three weeks before the end of the choir season. The books are then gone over carefully to see if the written work has been done and how neatly; to check attendance records against the official roll; and to insert a final report page.

This final page is addressed to the chorister and the parents. It thanks them for their help during the season and wishes them a refreshing vacation. It also carries a rating (Ex = exceptional, S = satisfactory, U = unsatisfactory) on co-operation, vocal progress, choir book (neatness, completeness) , and special study. In addition, it summarizes the chorister's attendance record as to number of times present, excused absences, and unexcused absences.

The choir book is returned to the chorister at the last rehearsal of the season.

BIBLIOGRAPHY

Symbolism

F. R. Webber, *Church Symbolism.* J. H. Jansen, 1938.

Thomas Albert Stafford, *Christian Symbolism in the Evangelical Churches.* Abingdon Press, 1942.

Friedrich Rest, *Our Christian Symbolism.* Christian Education Press, 1954.

Helen Stuart Griffith, *The Sign Language of Our Faith.* Morehouse-Gorham Co., Inc., 1947.

Frank E. Wilson, *An Outline of Christian Symbolism.* Morehouse-Gorham Co., Inc., 1938.

Interfaith Study

Florence Mary Fitch, *One God — The Ways We Worship Him.* Lothrop, Lee & Shepard Co., Inc., 1944.

Grace W. McGavran, *We Gather Together.* Friendship Press, 1941.

Sister Mary Ambrose, *My Gift to Jesus.* D. B. Hansen and Sons.

Harold A. Pfeiffer, *The Catholic Picture Dictionary.* Catholic Manufacturing Company, 1948.

Irving J. Rosenbaum and Oscar Tarcor, *Your Neighbor Celebrates.* Anti-Defamation League of B'nai B'rith, 1951.

Great Christians

Clyde Robert Bulla, *Song of St. Francis.* The Thomas Y. Crowell Co., 1952.

May McNeer and Lynd Ward, *John Wesley.* Abingdon Press, 1951.

———, *Martin Luther.* Abingdon Press, 1953.

Erica Anderson, *The World of Albert Schweitzer.* Harper & Brothers, 1955.

THE JUNIOR HIGH CHOIRS

Looking at it from the long-view standpoint, the junior high choirs are the most important choirs of the church. If the children of twelve, thirteen, and fourteen years of age learn to love the church and to take an active part in its life and work, in all probability they will not depart from the church in later life. Children of this age like to take part in public activities. They like to feel that they are needed. They like to feel that they are important. And they *are* important to the permanent progress of the church.

If it is going to appeal to this age, the choir program must be demanding, interesting, and constructive. This age is the biggest challenge to the director. His choir system will stand or fall in the intermediate choirs. They require his very best efforts as a choral director, music instructor, voice teacher, psychologist, and religious leader. As a choral director he must be more than a time beater; the director must guide the children into sincere interpretation of worthy music. As a music instructor he must teach the children the fundamentals of music in such an interesting, yet thorough, way that an adequate foundation is laid. As a voice teacher he must guide, guard, and develop the most delicate musical instrument. As a psychologist he will interest the youth in the choir program by being interested in them and their concerns. That is, children are interested in themselves, their birthdays, their school activities, their homes, their sports, and their hobbies. The director must become genuinely interested in these too. As a leader he must interpret spirituality to them. They should want to be Christians because of what they see in their director.

APPLICANTS

Most of the members of these choirs will come by promotion from the junior choir. Others will offer themselves because the parents have heard the choirs and feel that choral training will be good for their child. Still others will come because they are friends of choristers. The director who really wants to build his choir will not wait for children to come to him. He will ring doorbells and make phone calls and meet with their organized group that he may " by all means save some."

He should hear every applicant sing privately, even though he had the child in a younger choir. The candidate should be tested for naturalness of voice quality, a musical ear, memory span, and range. Posture and breathing should be noted and corrections suggested if necessary.

In this interview the director will be able to become acquainted with each child, his interests and abilities. A record should be kept of his address, place in school, birthday, musical studies, if any, and other information that will aid in the understanding and helping of the child. A birthday letter to each child is much appreciated and is good public relations.

Boys and Girls — Together or Separate?

It will be found expedient to separate the boys and girls at this age. They seem to work better in their own choirs. The problems of teaching will be simplified by having two choirs. The two choirs may sing the same music and sing together in public, but they should be treated as two distinct and independent units.

VOICE TRAINING

All that was suggested in the chapter on the junior choir regarding voice training is equally applicable to these choirs. The fundamentals of voice production must be insisted upon. More extensive vocalization may be done, though elaborate exercises are never necessary. If the director has a clear mental conception of the right tone for children's voices, he will work patiently and diligently to achieve it.

PART SINGING

The director will wish to perform some two- or possibly three-part music with the choirs. He may prepare for it by two-part vocal exercises. The following vocalises will serve as suggestions.

Sing chiefly on ōō.
Transpose within
the comfortable
range of the
voices.

Sing chiefly on ōō.
Transpose within
a third each way.

Divide the choir
into two sections
for all this part
vocalizing. Every-
one should have
training on sing-
ing both first and
second parts.

Continue the ōō
vowel sound.
However, blend
to *oh, aw, ah, ā, ē*
occasionally. Use
complete words if
you wish: *whom,
home, laud,
psalm, name,
thee.*

From this type of
vocalizing it is
but a step to the
singing of rounds.

The regular singing of rounds will lead to independence of parts. The children will find them fun as well.

When it is desired to divide the choirs for permanent two-part singing, several things have to be considered. As a rule, the older children should sing the second part. If possible all thirteen-year-olds should have a year's experience singing harmony before leaving this choir. The children with richest voice qualities should be in the second part. Those singing second will need to have a musical ear. They must be able to hear the under part when the melody is sung. The children who have had some piano instruction or other musicianship training will probably best be able to sing the harmony.

ADOLESCENT BOY'S VOICE

When the inexperienced director is reading oft-quoted books on the child voice as part of his preparation for the training of the boy choir, he will doubtless run into conflicting statements as to the so-called " break." He may read:

" Directly a boy shows any of the signs [of the break in the voice], his singing should absolutely cease, and he should be told to use even his talking voice as little and as gently as possible." [5]

Or he may read:

" It is, however, the height of folly to permit the voice to break when it can be trained down so easily. The boy may, nay, should sing all the time the change is taking place." [6]

In the light of these opinionated statements, the young director may feel at a loss as to how to proceed. Such a dilemma was shared by the writer when in 1934 he had

occasion to consult Elizabeth Van Fleet Vosseller, Founder
and Director of the Flemington (New Jersey) Children's
Choir School. She said, in essence, "We keep the boys
singing through the ' break ' by having them sing lightly
and only the notes most comfortable for them." The writer
has taken this statement, and the suggestions of John J.
Dawson in the book previously mentioned, as the basis for
his boy training. This procedure is unhesitatingly recommended.[7]

The problem of the change in the boy voice has been
discussed in this chapter because the director may expect
the signs of adolescence to appear in a few boys as early as
twelve; in others they may not appear until several years
later.[8] If the boy's voice is still light and high at fourteen,
it may be considered best for him to stay in the boys' choir.
At the time his voice changes, he should be put in the
senior high choir. Age is not the only consideration for
promotion to the young people's choir.

Adolescent Girl's Voice

Though there is almost as much change in the girl and
her voice as adolescence approaches, the vocal problems
involved are not so great. As the girl develops physically,
her voice takes on more depth and maturity; the range,
however, does not change so drastically as in a boy's voice.
Some girls' voices will lower to an alto range, but a majority will show only a change in quality.

Musicianship Training

Musicianship development must be continued in these
choirs. The primary elements of sight reading must be in-

stilled; more extensive ear training and interval teaching should be done. By the time the children have had three years in these choirs they should have a good knowledge of reading music.

In teaching hymns and anthems to intermediates, some of the methods suggested for junior choirs may still be employed. The twelve- to fourteen-year-old choristers will read the words and to some extent the music, probably more by position than by interval. Thus teaching by rote will not be necessary. One method of saving time when learning two-part music is by having a divided rehearsal. If both a director and an accompanist are used, each may take a part of the choir for sectional rehearsals, working in different rooms simultaneously. If the director is also the accompanist, he should have the help of an assistant for such rehearsals.

The director will probably find that the boys do not " pick up " the music so readily as do the girls. It takes them longer to learn the melody, to learn parts, and to memorize. This is apt to disturb the director unless he understands that tests have shown that at this age the boy is about a year and a half behind the girl in mental attainment. If they are in the same choir, the girls will be bored by the slowness of the boys, the boys will be embarrassed and discouraged by the swiftness of the girls. This is probably the strongest argument for two separate choirs of this age.

THE REHEARSAL

" Every rehearsal should be interesting but businesslike, as it is used for work only. If your material is thoroughly in hand, and you are definite in knowing what you want, it is generally obtained." [9] Much that was written regarding rehearsal procedure in the chapter on the junior choir can be used for these choirs. However, these children, being a little older, can concentrate on one point somewhat longer. The use of choir books as described in the preceding chapter has been found to be a good way to present material to the choirs.

As suggested for the junior choir, it is highly desirable that accurate records of the junior high choir's members be kept. Be exacting in your demands as to regularity, punctuality, and discipline. You are never being kind to a child to let him get by with slipshod work. Be uncompromisingly fair to all choristers. They will respect you if you handle all details in a businesslike manner.

SINGING IN PUBLIC

Both boy and girl choirs of this junior high age are capable of creditable, spiritual singing in the public worship service. They can be taught the music for a service so that their singing of it will in every way be satisfactory. They can be instructed in the meaning of the various parts of the ritual so that their leadership will be intelligent. They can be trained in the manners becoming to ministers in song so that their conduct in the service is exemplary. However, they should not be expected to sing in services more often than once in six weeks on one rehearsal a week. If it is possible to have twice as many rehearsals, they may sing a little more frequently. Children memorize so readily that in all probability they will have the music " by heart " by the time the director feels that it is thoroughly prepared. This being the case, the holding of a piece of music will be both superfluous and distracting. Choirs of the age under discussion like to be more active than a service once in six weeks will allow. It is well to arrange other times and places for them to sing, repeating anthems sung in church. They may sing for various church school departments or for other groups of the church. They may occasionally go to another church to sing or to a hospital or home. A well-trained children's choir is worth hearing; opportunities should be made for them to appear in public.

The junior highs are at an impressionable age. Imprints made on a child are lifelong — nay, eternity-long. The director, realizing this, can but humbly bow his head and plead for guidance.

REPERTOIRE AND HELPS FOR CHILDREN'S AND JUNIOR HIGH CHOIRS

REPERTOIRE

Before selecting any music, the director should ponder this question: What is the ultimate purpose of children's choirs? The music he selects will reflect his answer to this query. If the director decides that the real object is the development of Christian character through a musical means, it will be apparent in the high quality of words and music used. In the following discussion, constant reference is made to children's choirs; but the materials and procedures recommended are intended for junior high unchanged voices as well.

Hymn Selection

The first consideration in repertoire is the selection of hymns to be taught the children. Hymns should form at least a third of the study of the choir. The children's conception of the church, of its doctrines and beliefs, and of their responsibility to God and man will be more readily understood from hymns than from sermons. It is the director's responsibility to teach hymns that mold the children's lives to the highest ideals of Christian life and faith. No hymn with cheap, unscriptural words or catchy, secular tune will accomplish this. Select your hymn repertoire for the season before your choral year starts. Choose hymns from the authorized hymnal of your denomination; choose hymns appropriate for the seasons of the year; choose hymns that the children will sing throughout a lifetime of Christian worship; choose hymns that will build character; and choose hymns that will complement the teaching in the children's departments of the church school.

Anthem Selection

In selecting the anthems for the children's choirs, words and music must both be carefully considered. They must each have merit, and they must also be well adapted one to the other. The words do not need to be directly taken from the Scriptures or even from Scriptural paraphrases, though on the whole this is recommended. Neither do they need to come from the established liturgy of the church, but if they do, this will insure their worth. They should, however, be cast in the form and meaning of Sacred Writ. Like the hymn, they should reflect the highest ideals of Christian life and faith.

The music should unfold the meaning of the words. It should be well within the range and abilities of the singers. It should be mostly diatonic. It should be free from the idioms of secular music. The music should be interesting and challenging to the children and in itself have permanent value.

In building a library, have an eye to future needs. Some directors make it a point to purchase music in two and three parts even though the choir at the time may be doing only unison singing. Then in a year or two, when two-part singing is being done, some material will already be in the library. This method of library-building may be carried to the point of purchasing regular mixed four-part anthems which the young people's or adult choir might later use. Then, too, younger choirs may use the melody of some simple types of anthems that the older choirs have used. The director will often be called upon to use his ingenuity and originality in arranging and adapting hymns and anthems for his own use.

Any music worth purchasing is worth taking care of. A good librarian with tape and time can make the music much more durable. Choristers will appreciate neatly bound or hinged copies of music.

Anthem Collections

Most music houses have published in book form some of their best anthems for children's voices. This, one would conclude, would give to the choirs a supply of good, usable music at but a part of the cost of buying the individual anthems. The economy is not so great as might be anticipated, however, for the director may find that only a portion of the contents of any one book will be of use to him. However, the publishing houses have in many instances made the contents of their anthem books available as separate octavo numbers.

The following inexpensive collections of anthems for children's voices are recommended to the director for perusal. In them he is likely to find many numbers of beauty and usefulness which he will want to obtain.

The Junior Choir Anthem Book, edited by Carl and Lenore Mueller. Edwin H. Morris & Co., Inc. All for unison voices, with optional alto.

The Junior Chorister, edited by Carl Mueller. Harold Flammer, Inc. 2 vols. For two-part treble voices.

Hymns and Anthems, edited by David Hugh Jones. Carl

Fischer, Inc. 3 sets. Unison and two parts.

Junior Choir Anthem Book, edited by John Holler. The H. W. Gray Company, Inc. Book I (two parts) and Book II (unison).

Anthems for the Junior Choir. The Westminster Press. Books 1, 2, and 3. Unison and two-part, with responsive readings and selections for choric speech.

Songs from Luke, texts by Demarest and music by Bristol. Canyon Press, Inc. Director's Edition and Junior Edition.

New Carols and Songs for Children, by William Grime. Carl Fischer, Inc. For young children. Fifty-four compositions.

Carols and Songs, by William Grime. Carl Fischer, Inc. For primary and junior voices. New material, not included in above collection. *Christmas Carols,* Series I; *Christmas Carols,* Series II. *Hymns and Anthems,* by William Grime. Carl Fischer, Inc. For primary and junior voices. *Teachings of Jesus,* Series I; *Finding God Through Nature,* Series I; *Hymns of Prayer and Praise,* Series I.

We Go to Church, by Marshall and Montgomery. Carl Fischer, Inc. Fifteen excellent songs for junior choir, unison with some two- and three-part passages. Interestingly illustrated.

The Choir Mothers' Guild

Of major importance for the smooth handling of a series of youth choirs is a well-organized, active group of lay-women, often called the Choir Mothers' Guild. Such a group can be the left arm of the director, the keystone in the arch that supports his program, and the oil that calms the troubled moments just ahead of a service. It is such an important unit in the choir system that the director should spend any amount of time necessary to get it well organized and functioning. As the activities of the choirs develop, the director will realize this time was profitably spent.

Organization

The first step in organizing this guild is to find the right person for head choir mother. This woman should have a " way " with children, a love for the church, an understanding of and a sympathy with the aims and dreams of the director. She should have the ability to get others to work with her, and she should have time enough to administer the plans successfully. After conferences with the pastor and others who may know the potential of the church membership, the right person can be found. Such a person may or may not have a child in the choir system.

After the head choir mother is procured, she should select an assistant. The two then meet with the director to go over the personnel of each choir, selecting mothers to ask to be responsible for each of the groups. The number of choir mothers needed for any choir depends on its size and on the responsibilities the director wishes the mothers to assume. In general the younger choirs need more help, possibly one mother to every ten children; in the older children's choirs, one mother to twenty children is sufficient.

What the Guild Does

When the roster has been completed, it is well for the director to meet with the entire Guild. At this meeting he should explain his philosophy of music in the church, the reason he believes in children's choirs, and what he is trying to accomplish in the lives of the children. He should try to inspire the mothers with the opportunity and to challenge them with the responsibility. At this meeting the director should outline just what obligations he wants the Guild to assume. It may well be that the following will be among these obligations:

Assist at each rehearsal in the taking of attendance, helping with wraps, and making the choir room attractive with flowers, pictures, and seasonal decorations;

Make telephone calls to absentees and report to the

director, make calls on sick members which the director will also do, and be on the lookout for new members;

Take charge of fitting and assigning the vestments at the beginning of the season, see that the vestments are kept clean and in good repair, help to teach the choristers how to care for their vestments and to have pride in them, see that the vestments are in the proper place and ready for use when the choir is to appear in public;

On singing days, help the children with their vesting, assist in the lining up for the processional, and sit near them during the service;

After service compliment them if they have sung effectively and if their conduct has been commendable, and see that the vestments are put away properly;

Plan and carry out some parties or outings during the year. Some of the things that can be done include: skating parties, hobby shows, fishing trips, boat trips, attending professional or college sports events, concerts, musical movies, television shows. Occasionally there should be "surprise" refreshments at the end of the rehearsal.

All these are helpful, and many of them are indispensable for the best results with children's choirs. The Choir Mothers' Guild can do them all, thereby relieving the director of many details and making a significant contribution to the ministry of music program.

Fathers Too

Why exclude the fathers from such an important group? Many church schools are finding that couples as teachers of children's classes can do a better piece of work than either could do alone. They share the teaching, share the record-keeping, share the supervising of all activities of the class. It may be sagacious on the part of the director to take a tip from the church school and enlist the help of both fathers and mothers in the work of the Guild.

There are activities of the Guild, such as some of those suggested above, that men perform better than women. Also it is good for the choristers, particularly the boys, to know that men are interested in the work of the choirs.

THE HIGH SCHOOL CHOIR

The high school choir is an adult choir. It is not a children's organization. To develop a choir of young people the director must have this hypothesis. If he embraces this theory, it will influence everything he does with the choir. It will affect his selection of singers, his voice training of them, the way he handles the group, and the music he uses.

THAT DIFFICULT AGE

Fifteen through seventeen, the age recommended for this choir, is a critical period in life. In these years new influences are acting upon the young people. The strongest new force is a sudden physical development. The situations encountered in the high school are difficult. The heterodoxy occasionally met with in the classroom is perplexing. Adults' proverbial misunderstanding of youth is discouraging. It is at this juncture in life that it is particularly necessary for the church to hold its young people. They need the stabilizing influence of the church life and worship. It is here that a choir can be of help. There are many young people interested in music, and through the choir they can be retained in the church.

72

The Choir Program

The choir program must be so attractive and challenging that the young people will want to be members. The choir must offer something that they truly want. What do they want? Briefly stated, they want to learn how to sing better; they want to sing good music expressively; they want worthy responsibility; they want to be important; they want to be near the opposite sex. Show them how the choir offers these things.

Recruiting

After a graded choir system has been in operation for even a few years, promotions from the younger choirs will probably fill the vacancies in the high school choir each season. If not, personal contacts with musically inclined young people will be necessary.

Up to this high school age it is advisable to work through the parents to arouse the child's interest in the choir. At this fifteen- to eighteen-year age deal directly with the prospective chorister. The young people resent being contacted through the parents. Try to get the leaders of the youth life of the church. The natural leaders will influence the followers. There will seldom be a problem of getting enough girls for the choir, but it may be more difficult to secure sufficient boys. If the athletes of the church are in the choir, this will attract the boys. Spot the idol of the boys, and work on him for membership in the choir. At this age certain boys will want to join if certain girls are members.

AUDITIONS

The director should hear each applicant sing individually. It is best to do this at a private interview. The director should test as to voice quality and part; the amount of musical knowledge should be determined. The rules of membership and what will be expected of the singer can be explained and his co-operation enlisted.

In this choir it is best to divide into the regular four parts: soprano, alto, tenor, and bass. It is not always easy to assign the voices of young people fifteen to eighteen years of age to the correct part. In about two thirds of the applicants the parts they should sing will be obvious. Never, however, take an individual's word for it; test him yourself. Test him for such things as range, quality, and ability to sustain high or low tones. The remaining third, on the other hand, are not easily placed. Even the most experienced voice teachers are sometimes wrong in their diagnoses. Young voices, because of rapid physical development, should be tested often.

There are several guideposts that the director will find helpful in assigning these voices to the correct parts:

1. The natural speaking voice will be an indication. With certain individuals it is difficult to tell the natural pitch of the speaking voice. Nervousness may alter the level of the speech, but when the individual is calm he may reveal his normal voice.

2. The unrestricted singing voice, even though the range may be short, will indicate a tenor or bass, soprano or alto quality. At times it takes several interviews with instruction in posture, breathing, jaw freedom, and correct articulation to find the free singing voice.

3. The ability to sustain a high or low tone is an indication of the correct voice. Many singers can sing a high

tone while vocalizing a rapid staccato arpeggio, but only a
tenor or soprano can easily sustain a high tone.

4. It is only a general rule, but one worth considering,
that as an average basses and altos are several pounds
heavier than sopranos and tenors. Physical appearance is
an indication. The lower voices are generally from larger,
heavier frames; the higher voices, from smaller bodies.
You may quickly recall notable exceptions, but remember
that they are the exceptions and not the rule.

5. The most reliable test to determine the various voices
is called by Herbert Witherspoon "the lift of the
breath." [10] He explains this phenomenon as follows:

" As we pass out of the easy speaking range of the voice, the
breath action or support increases somewhat, thus preserving
correct vocal position, the vocal organs exaggerate their move-
ments for the higher pitches, and at one particular note in the
scale the sound seems to gain in facial resonance, and the vowel
modifies slightly.

" Generally speaking, this note is C♯ or D in sopranos and
tenors, B in baritones and mezzo-sopranos, A in high basses
and contraltos, G in low basses and contraltos."

The male voice is, of couse, an octave below the female
voice. This method has been found highly accurate with
voices that have no glaring faults. If you find " throati-
ness " of tone or " hootiness " or other bad vocal habits,
these must be eliminated before the young singer will reveal the true " lift " in the voice. The director should
make many tests with voices before he says positively what
part a voice should sing.

UNCHANGED VOICE

If there are boys, eligible as far as age is concerned, who
want to sing in the high school choir but whose voices have

not changed, they may still be used. These voices belong in the tenor section. They will sing in the lower parts of their unchanged voice, which will be in the easy range of the tenors. The quality will be different, but it will do no particular harm. If it is a question of sacrificing the quality slightly or losing the interest of the boy, of course the former is preferable. As the voice changes, the young man will be placed in whichever section he belongs in.

Group voice training must be done with this choir. As stated previously, the young people should be treated as adults.

CHOOSING THE ANTHEM

Use anthems that are on a high plane. The young people know good music from cheap music. They know good poetry from inferior poetry. Their tastes are often on a loftier level than we think. Good music does not necessarily mean difficult music. Some of the finest anthems are not involved musically.

Do not sneer at unison anthems. Better an expressive unison than a labored four-part anthem. It may be found advisable to use three-part material (soprano, alto, and one part for the men, baritone) if the choir is short on men or if the choristers are not experienced at part singing. If three-part material is desired, the following collections should be examined. Many of the anthems contained in these collections are obtainable separately.

Anthems for the Youth Choir — Book I, edited by W. Lawrence Curry. The Westminster Press. Twenty-two anthems for S.A.B. and S.A.T.B.

The Gateway, edited by Mathew Lundquist. E. C. Schirmer, Inc. Twenty anthems for S.A.B.

Junior Choir Anthem Book — Book III, compiled by John
Holler. The H. W. Gray Co., Inc. Ten anthems for S.A.B.
Schirmer's Favorite Sacred Choruses, arranged by Carl F.
Mueller. G. Schirmer, Inc. Fifteen anthems for S.A.B.

As soon as there is sufficient balance and musical development, use four-part anthems.

SINGING IN PUBLIC

The high school choir is the connecting link between
the children's choirs and the principal adult choir of the
church. This choir sings more often in public than the
children's choirs, but it will not be expected to sing so
many services as the adult choir. It should sing often in
young people's meetings and in other church functions. It
will be greatly stimulated by an occasional trip to sing
outside the church.

Give the young people worth-while responsibility, and
they will rise to the occasion. Treat them as grownups,
and they will respond as such. Lavish your best efforts on
this choir. It is worth it!

8

THE ADULT CHOIR

The principal choir of a church and congregation, which Sunday by Sunday leads the people in the offering of their sacrifices of praise to God, is perpetuating a many-centuries-old line of singers set apart as ministers in song. In each generation there have been those whose special gifts of voice, musical inclination, and temperament fitted them for this calling. Though figures are not available to support this supposition, there probably has never been a generation when so many people were regularly occupied in singing the praises of God in choirs as this generation. Despite the fact that in some parts of the world public worship, with its clerical and musical ministrations, has been banned, the churches of the countries having religious freedom have greatly increased the numbers of their choristers. The so-called volunteer choirs, as distinguished from the paid or professional choirs, have in the last half century become more numerous and better trained. This growth has paralleled the revival of worship which is evident throughout all Protestantism. This revivification is in the ascendancy, and we are sure to find that in the coming years the quality and number of choirs will continue to increase.

Purpose

The main adult choir of a church has several objectives. These aim in two directions: that is, outward to assist the worshipers and inward to enrich the singers themselves.

The choir's first function is to lead congregational singing. By adequately preparing and rendering the hymns, the choir can greatly assist the worshipers in expressing their prayer and praise. The second function is to minister to the congregation through the interpretation of great thought expressed in poetry and music, thought that is clothed in a form that it is beyond the capabilities of the congregation as a whole to express. This is the interpretation of sacred musical art: anthems, cantatas, oratorios, and the like. Both functions should be in evidence in all churches. However, in some places one function may be needed more than the other.

The choir has other purposes also. Some of these are directed toward the singers themselves. Singing in a choir, with its regular contacts with ennobling poetic and musical ideas and regular attendance at divine worship, should build high moral and spiritual values into the lives of the choristers. In many churches a renewed emphasis is being given to stewardship, a stewardship that embraces the idea of time and talent as well as financial resources. Singing in the choir gives the opportunity to discharge this phase of one's obligation to God.

In most churches the choir is placed in such a position that it is in eye-range of the congregation throughout the worship hour. This is not all bad if the choir realizes its opportunity and carefully discharges its duty to be leaders in " visual worship." Most church members have not been taught attitudes that aid worship. By seeing the choir stand uniformly, sing spiritedly, bow during prayer reverently, sit during interludes quietly, listen during Scripture readings intently, and concentrate on the sermon thoughtfully, the people in the pews will observe what their attitudes should be.

THE ADULT CHORISTER

It takes a particular type of person to make a good chorister. He must have a number of distinctive qualities. He must have a good voice and musicianship and a desire to develop both. He must have a love of the church and an eagerness to serve it. He must have interest in choral music. He must have physical vigor and mental alertness. He must have those extremely important twin virtues, dependability and loyalty. He must be able and willing to lose his individuality of voice and personality in the greater voice and personality of a choir.

THE CHOIR PROGRAM

But what does the church choir have to offer a person with such desirable qualifications? The singer has a right to ask, "If I give my time and services to the church through its choir, what does the church give in exchange?" It is not selfishness that prompts such a question. Compensation is a law of life; it holds good in the choir loft as well as elsewhere. The serious singer seems to want four things from a church choir; he has a right to expect them too. If the director hopes to build a good choir he must offer an opportunity for self-expression, self-advancement, social contacts, and service to the church.

Self-expression

The person with vocal gifts finds in singing more than just a pastime. He finds an opportunity to express himself, to give utterance to his emotional nature. Singing, for him, is an essential part of life. Few, however, have the ability to develop into successful concert artists and thus satisfy that desire. It is here that the church choir steps in and offers that emotional release that the singer is seeking. W. G. McNaught refers to all choral groups when he says, " The obvious advantage of collective singing is that individuals possessing only ordinary musical gifts are, under skilled training, enabled to achieve artistic results that afford great satisfaction to both performers and auditors." [11] However, the director must do more than beat time to satisfy his singers; he must lead them in the paths of sincere devotional interpretation for their musical souls' sake.

Self-advancement

For the serious person, learning must not stop when the formal schooling is over; he must continue his intellectual development. The serious singer wants to better his own voice and broaden his understanding and appreciation of music. Singing in a choir must be one form of adult education. The more that can be offered in the way of voice instruction, musicianship study, and musical appreciation, the greater the appeal to the conscientious singer.

Social Contacts

Man is so constituted that it is extremely difficult for him to " live alone and like it." Social contacts are almost a necessity with him. Contacts with one whose ideas and ambitions are like his are mutually enjoyable. Thus when singers join their voices in song there is a kinship created that does not find its parallel in many phases of life. This does not refer to " socials," but to the sociality of singing together. Two of the most intimate relationships in life, outside the family circle, are created when we sing together and when we break bread together. Jesus often used one or the other of these situations to expound his deepest thoughts to his disciples. At the Last Supper they both broke bread together and sang together. When you meet with a group of singers twice a week or more for eight or nine months of the year and join your hearts and voices with but a single idea — the praise of God — a mutual understanding and affection are bound to develop, and this enriches life.

Service to the Church

The person who has the aforementioned qualities and who is interested in adult learning and in the expression of his inner self through music doubtless will desire to be of service to the institution that has fathered the arts and fostered education — the church. Such a person will have an inherent feeling of thankfulness for the gift of song which he possesses. He will want to render worship and gratitude to its Giver. The church choir offers this opportunity.

RECRUITING

In a church that has a graded choir system, some of the applicants for the adult choir will come from the young people's choir. These young people, having been trained by the same leadership and having grown up to the adult choir age, logically should desire membership in the senior choir. Because of this, they should be given the preference as vacancies occur. Others will apply for membership because they are attracted to the opportunities the choir offers. Some will make application because of the enthusiasm shown by a choir-member friend. Still other prospects may have to be ferreted out from a suggested list given by the pastor. The choir director must not wait for people to come to him. He should inquire about each new family that joins the church. He should learn if there are potential choir members in the family. Then he should go to them to sell his product. The director must learn to ring doorbells.

The Interview

The director should have a private interview with each applicant. The aspirant should first be made to talk about himself and his preparation and qualifications. This will do several things. It will give an opportunity to study the personality and the speaking voice and to learn of the candidate's previous training and experience in voice work.

Next the director should hear the applicant sing to determine his degree of musical proficiency, to test his ear, and to determine the tone quality of his voice and the part he should sing. Never take a person's word for the part he should sing. Make your own tests.

There are many tenors singing baritone just because they have never developed their voices. They are of little use as baritones, for they are singing out of the natural center of their voices and will probably force their middle and low tones. There are altos singing soprano because they think it is the most important part. Such voices will make it impossible to achieve a blend of the soprano section.

Balance

The ideal is to take members into the choir in only the right proportion to insure a balance of voices. Unfortunately this can rarely be done. If there is a large number of applicants, this point will probably take care of itself. The balance will not be in numbers, that is, there will not be an even number of sopranos, altos, tenors, and basses. There will, however, be a balance in tone. It does not take so many altos as sopranos to have a balance in a choir; neither does it take so many tenors as basses.

Noble Cain has consoling words in this observation: " It even seems as though the Divine Creator made tenors a scarce article so that overambitious conductors would not put too many in choruses! Indeed, a few tenors will balance many times their number of basses. Their tones are more penetrating and higher in range." [12]

If the choir is small, balance will have to be achieved either by " shuttle " voices (high baritones who can sing tenor, or low altos who can reinforce the tenor, low sopranos who can double as altos, and so on) or by using music with fewer parts. One of the ingredients of all art forms is balance. Thus we should work for it in our choirs.

TEACHING VOICE PRODUCTION
TO ADULT CHORISTERS

The principles of voice production can be taught to a choir through two approaches: physical and phonetic.

PHYSICAL APPROACH

All tone-producing instruments have three essential elements. These may be called the motor, the vibrator, and the resonator.

The motor is the energy-supplying agent, the muscles which do the work. The vibrator receives the action of the motor and is thereby made to oscillate rapidly, setting up regular sound waves. When these sound waves strike the eardrum the sensation we call tone is produced. The resonator is anything that amplifies the sound or that vibrates sympathetically with the sound, thereby reinforcing the original tone and giving it a richer quality and greater carrying power.

In piano-playing, the muscles of the fingers and arms form the motor, the strings are the vibrators, and the sounding board is the resonator. In the violin, the muscles of the bowing arm form the motor, the strings form the vibrator, and the case forms the resonator. In playing a trumpet, the breath-controlling muscles of the player form the motor, the closely approximated and intensified lips form the vibrator, the tube of the instrument forms the resonator. In the human instrument, the muscles of inhalation and exhalation may be considered the motor. The vocal cords, or, more correctly called, the vocal lips, located in the larynx, are the vibrators. The cavities of the throat and head and the bony structure of the chest and head are the resonators. In the human tone-producing instrument there is a fourth element involved: this is articulation.

Stripping the act of singing to the basic processes, we find that air comes into the lungs because space is provided for it by the lowering of the diaphragm and the enlarging just above the waistline all around the body. A singer does not " take breath "; he provides the space by expansion, and breath takes possession of him. The mind now calls for a pitch and a vowel sound.[13] The vocal cords are involuntarily drawn to a certain tension, and the articulating muscles prepare the vowel shape. The air now starts from the lungs, and the phonation is established. The energy of the air expended sets and keeps the vocal lips in vibration. This oscillation sets up sound waves which come up into the throat and mouth cavities. These sound waves are amplified or reinforced by the cavities of the head and throat and the bony structures of the head and chest. The sound waves are affected by the shape of the mouth and throat cavities in another way. The oral shape determines the vowel. A slight change in the contour of these cavities will result in a vowel change. If the vowel sound is suppressed or momentarily stopped by some action of the tongue or lips the result is a consonant.

Of these four parts of the singing process — motor, vibrator, resonator, and articulator — the singer has direct control over only two, the motor and the articulators. He cannot by direct action put the vocal cords in any particular position. This must be done by the mind calling for a certain pitch. Within their natural range, the vocal cords will respond to the mind if there is no abnormal physical condition present. All the singer can do to control the vibrator is done by a right mental concept.

Certain exercises may aid and intensify resonance (chiefly exercises using *m, n,* and *ng* consonants and the $\overline{oo}$ vowel) , but one can do little, if anything, to develop the resonators themselves.

The singer has direct control over two of the essentials in tone production, namely, the motor or the inhalation of air and the articulation or the pronouncing of vowels and consonants. In corroboration of this, one might quote one of the early *bel canto* teachers:

" He who knows how to breathe and how
to pronounce knows how to sing."

In teaching voice, the first consideration is the development of the motor muscles or the proper inhalation of air. The person who would sing must first learn how best to fill his lungs. This can be done only under the condition established by correct posture. This correct posture may be gained easily from the idea of sitting or standing " tall." Let the singer imagine a book balanced upon the head, then that he is standing or sitting with the book as high as possible. This straightens the spine, brings in the chin, and with head back, lifts the chest, broadens the ribs, draws in the abdominal wall slightly, and allows free action of the diaphragm for inhalation. If one is sitting, the hips must be well back in the chair, but the back must not touch the chair. If standing, there will be an imaginary straight line dropped from the highest part of the head through the shoulders, through the hips to the balls of the feet. Insist on this posture. With this position, " drink in the breath through parted lips, rather slowly at first, with the sensation that you are inflating the body to the lowest point of the torso. Your feeling should be that the lower throat opens to its capacity and that the body expands in a lateral ' spread ' at front, back, and sides." [14] In this way one may best and most completely fill the lungs.

A great aid to the correct physical preparation which will produce good tone is the right mental attitude. The mood desired is happiness and confidence; this will give physical buoyancy. Man functions most efficiently when he is gay, optimistic, and joyful. The muscles that co-operate to produce phonation cannot be forced to function properly; they must be prevailed upon or beguiled, as it were. The director who has about himself this buoyancy, who knows how to put a choir at ease and in a confident frame of mind by a calming smile, who senses when to say a word of encouragement and praise, can do much to establish and maintain a good singing mood in his group.[15]

PHONETIC APPROACH

After the singers have been taught correct posture, full and complete inhalation of air, and after they have sensed the importance of a lighthearted mood, they should be introduced to English phonetics.

Phonetics is the science of the sounds of speech. Through applying phonetic understanding, bad vocal habits may be overcome and correct vocal habits may be established. This will result in accurate and understandable choral diction. If the choristers are told to raise the uvula, or to lower the larynx, or to arch or groove the tongue, or to try to put any muscle in a particular position, it will lead to tension and defeat the purpose of the instruction. If, however, the chorister is asked to imitate a phonetic sound, the muscles will be induced to act correctly.

Many of the glaring faults of amateur choral groups may be quickly remedied if the director understands and teaches phonetics. If he can illustrate the correct speech sounds he has a ready vehicle for the overcoming of many choral blemishes. If the choristers will imitate the sounds that are patterned for them, the director can lead them out of the forest of ugly tones made by poorly produced vowels and consonants and into the meadows of pleasant tones produced with good diction.

It is impossible through written words to illustrate the exact sounds of vowels and consonants. These must be taught orally. It is strongly recommended that the vocal director avail himself of this valuable means of voice teaching by himself becoming thoroughly familiar with all speech sounds and the method of articulating each. This can best be accomplished through personal study with a phonetician. It is preferable to study with one who is also a singer or a teacher of singing. In lieu of this, one should do extensive reading and studying.

The following books are recommended:

Webster's New International Dictionary, Second Edition, Unabridged. Guide to pronunciation.

~ William Henry P. Phyfe, *20,000 Words Often Mispronounced.* G. P. Putnam's Sons, 1937.

Sara M. Barbara, *Speech Education.* Little, Brown & Co., 1939.

Alexander Melville Bell, *Principles of Speech.* Volta Bureau, Washington, D. C., 1916.

The director will find that when basses and altos muffle their low tones, the illustration of a pure *ah* or *aw* mouth shape will help them to open the low voice and give a more pleasing sound. Stiff jaws should vocalize alternate *ah-ōō-ah-ōō* with a drastic jaw action. Rigid and incorrect tongues should be made to pronounce rapidly *nah-nah-lah-lah-tah-tah-dah-dah,* etc., without jaw action, and so on.

Vocal Consonants

Most sliding attacks will be corrected if the singers realize that certain consonant sounds call for pitch in their enunciation. These pitch consonants must be sung on the pitch given to the syllable in which they are found. Suppose the choir has the following phrase:

Sliding is bound to occur unless the choir is instructed as to the nature of these consonant sounds. *Th, L, s* (z) *, m, l,* all being consonants having pitch, must be sung on the pitch indicated for their syllable. In other words, a short, but nevertheless accurate, sound of *th* must be given on F before the vowel of the word; the sound of *l* must be sounded on C before the vowel, and so forth. These consonants requiring pitch will be sounded somewhere; if the choir is to sing cleanly, these consonants must be sounded on the right pitch. Instances of this kind will be found repeatedly in every anthem. Most of the slurring common in amateur choirs can be overcome if the director will insist on the right pitch for the following sounds: *m, n, ng, l, r, v, z, zh* (vision) *, th* (they) *, w* (won) *,* and *y* (yes) . These consonants must, however, be greatly reduced in length or even eliminated when singing high tones; otherwise they may interfere with good tone.

The Consonant R

The director will often have to cope with the guttural *r* sound. This repelling sound is the result of the tongue being drawn back in the throat, often to the point where the passage to the throat is nearly blocked off. If the *r* precedes a vowel, it must be sounded with the tip of the tongue forward in the mouth. If the meaning of the word suggests strength or action (such as " arise," " triumph," " praise," " rejoice," " run," " rage "), the *r* may be trilled or rolled. A much more difficult sound to handle is that which choristers often use in such words as " her," " Father," " earth," " world," " glory," " worship," " urge," " Lord," " forever." The sound of the *r* must not unduly affect the vowel. The tongue must lie still at the bottom of the mouth, the tip touching the lower teeth while the vowel sound is uttered. In correcting pronunciation faults, correct phonetic illustration to be copied by the singers is better than many words of explanation.

Vowel Modification

Many throaty or strident upper tones will be eliminated if the director understands and teaches the principle of vowel modification. As a soprano sings an ascending scale on an $\overline{oo}$ vowel, for instance, she will find it necessary to begin to lower the jaw (open the mouth) as she comes about to D (fourth line treble staff) if she wishes to sing with good tone. As she continues to ascend, passing F♯ and G, the true character of the $\overline{oo}$ will be lost, and the vowel will become about the sound of $\breve{u}$. Continuing the ascent, the vowel will brighten and be opened until it closely resembles *ah.* Some such modification takes place in all voices, though chiefly noticed in sopranos, and on all vowels. The vowels farthest away from *ŭ* in mouth and throat shape (that is, *ōo, ē, ā*) will start their modification lower than vowels which are near *ŭ* (such as *aw, ŏ, ĭ*) .[16]

One may say, " If this is the correct method of uttering vowels in the high voice, how can one ever get good diction on these tones? " The answer is, " He cannot." Fortunately, however, this is not too serious. Most composers, having understood this characteristic of high tones, indicate words for these tones that were previously used in the easy-pronouncing part of the voice. In choral music, composers have often used several parts in middle range while one part is in high range. Thus if one part cannot pronounce accurately, the others can.

Records of first-rate choruses and soloists should be listened to with an ear for vowel modification. It might be advisable to play records for the choir to point out certain modified vowels for them to pattern, such as:

Victor 11825   " Hallelujah Chorus," sung by the Royal Choral Society
                " And the Glory of the Lord " (*The Messiah*)
Victor 1817   " Lullaby," by Cyril Scott, sung by Kirsten Flagstad
Victor 15826   " O Sleep, Why Dost Thou Leave Me? " (Handel) , sung by Dorothy Maynor

A good choral blend of voices can never be obtained unless all voices are pronouncing a given word alike. If one voice pronounces " God " as if it were *Gawd,* another *Gahd,* another *Gord,* another *Guhd,* and another the correct sound, *Gŏd,* no blend will be possible. Again, accurate phonetic illustration by the director will bring the desired result.

Correct phonetics should be taught to a choir so that their accurate and scholarly pronunciation of the English language will make their singing beautiful, their words easily understood, and their interpretations effective.

Common Phonetic Errors

The most common errors in pronunciation may be catalogued as: substitution, omission, addition of sounds in syllables, and the overlapping of words in sentences. Since these errors are as common in singing as in speaking, this fourfold indictment makes them an excellent outline for the remainder of this discussion.

Substitution. Though we occasionally hear someone who should know better sing *tōon* when he means *tūne* or *Fawther* when *Father* is meant, the most common substitutions seem to be in unaccented syllables. How often we hear *heavun*, for *heaven*, *eternuty* for *eternity*, *beautuful* for *beautiful*, *Ameruca* for *America*, and so forth. Phyfe quotes Richard Grant White as saying, " It is in the delicate but firm utterance of the unaccented vowels with correct sound that the cultured person is most surely distinguished from the uncultured." [17] This quotation may aptly be paraphrased to read, " It is the correct pronunciation by his choir of the unaccented syllables that most surely distinguishes the cultured, painstaking director from the untutored or slovenly one."

Going over just one anthem (" This Glad Easter Day," by Dickinson) , I find these words which the careless singer might let slip: *heartbrokun, desolute, triumphunt, risun, livuth, promuse, strengthun, sucure, servuce.* You will notice that in all these words the natural vowel sound of short *uh* (so-called because it is the one most easily produced by the vocal organs) is the one that might be substituted for the correct vowel. The word " too " and similar words with the long $\overline{oo}$ sound give some people trouble to pronounce correctly. Among the various sounds that are substituted for the $\overline{oo}$ are $\breve{oo}$ and $\bar{e}$-$\overline{oo}$ as in "view." This careless pronunciation habit seems to be derived from the colloquial speech of some sections of the country, notably the South, and from the correct sounds in foreign languages carried into English.

Should sectional colloquialisms be allowed in the singing of a solo or anthem? The thoughtful director will say not. He will have several standard pronunciation dictionaries on his studio desk and consult them often. He will never present an anthem to his choir until he is sure of the correct English sounds of every syllable.

Omission. How often when a person is introduced to you do you find it necessary to ask for a repetition of the name! This is because the introducer has probably been slovenly in his pronunciation and has omitted sounds. Those most likely to be left off are the explosive consonants: *p, t, k, b, d, g, j.* In conversation you might understand the introducer, for you would have the context to help you. When, however, he carelessly pronounces isolated names or sentences, you are at a loss to understand him.

Most anthems are built on words that are not part of our ordinary conversation. The audience has no context to help it. The choir must mold each sentence without omissions if it wishes to be understood. Occasionally we find something of a fugal nature (see the latter part of Brahms's " Grant Unto Me the Joy of Thy Salvation ") where the words are but a vehicle for the utterance of vocal sounds. This is essentially instrumental music. However, the words of most anthems are meant to be understood.

Addition. The director who is careful in phonetics will guard against adding sounds that should not be there. As

Phyfe says, " It displays as much ignorance to introduce a sound that is superfluous as to neglect one that is requisite." [18] The obnoxious habit common with would-be dramatic singers is one form of addition. They add grunted *uh*'s to such words as *home, soon, song, live;* in fact, to most words ending in *m, n, ng, l,* or *v.* There may be an occasional high or truly emotional climax where the addition of *uh* would intensify the interpretative effect, but this device must be used with extreme caution.

Many amateur singers have the habit of sustaining both or the wrong parts of diphthongs. This is one form of addition, an addition in time value. When there are two vowel sounds that are used in one syllable, one is sustained to nearly the full value of the note; the other, given but a very short value. Thus, in such words as " thou," " now," the first sound, i.e., *ah,* is sustained; the second sound, $\overline{oo}$, is very short. The reader who does not have a complete understanding of this phase of phonetics is urged to study the key to pronunciation in a standard dictionary.

Overlapping. Some time ago my children were rehearsing a new anthem ("Here a Little Child I Stand," by Markham Lee) , and I had one child sing a section alone. This is what I heard: " O nour mea tan do nu sall." The phrase should have been: " On our meat and on us all." This is an extreme case of overlapping. Note that six of the seven words of the phrase start with vowels.

To eradicate this fusion of the last sound of one word with the vowel sound that opens the next, a slight break or stop is necessary. This stop should be but the completed pronunciation of the first sound and should in no way break the phrase line. It is entirely possible to do this, though it takes considerable practice. In most cases of overlapping we find the second word begins with a vowel sound; this is not always the case, however. Once a year we are admonished by some careless one to " be glad this sappy Christmas " when " this happy Christmas " is meant. Who is there who has not heard a choir start Gounod's anthem, " Sen doubt thy light," instead of " Send out," or the Goss Lenten favorite sung " sa vu sand hel pus " instead of " save us and help us "? Where is the congregation that has not sung " thi sour hymn of grateful praise " when they meant " this our hymn "? The psalmist instructed us to " let all men praise Him," not just the " tall " men, as so many singers say.

If the director can train his choir to sing without the common errors of substitution, omission, addition, and overlapping, he will have gone a long way toward bringing it into the very select group of choirs that sing the English language beautifully and in a way that can be understood.

If you cultivate the vowels, you will sing beautifully; if you honor the consonants you will sing distinctly.

AN APPROACH TO CHORAL
INTERPRETATION

EMOTIONAL TONE

Some principles of interpretation can be suggested to a choir through finding and using the right emotional tone. To explain, the director must determine the mood of the words and music and must guide the choir in the expression of that mood in such a way that the listeners will feel it. If this is done and the choir interprets sincerely, it will do away with the hesitation and apprehension of the singers. It will add a glow and warmth to the voices as well as to the faces. It will lift the singing above the mediocre level of most choral work.

The singing of poetry or prose is a process vastly different from conversation. In natural conversation everything is spontaneous. There are real reasons to say what is being said, and in all likelihood we are unconscious of the method of delivery. But when singing, we take another's words and music and try to make them our natural expression.

The choir may be asked to sing Whittier's:

" O brother man, fold to thy heart thy brother;
    Where pity dwells, the peace of God is there;
To worship rightly is to love each other,
    Each smile a hymn, each kindly deed a prayer."

In all probability there will be no one in the group who in his own conversation ever used any of these phrases. How then is the choir to project the feeling of the words; how is there to be any naturalness in their expression? A possible way is by likening the thought and feeling of these words to something in the experience of each chorister.

All spoken and sung words have both thought and feeling. Interpreters must be consistent. They must project both the idea and the emotion. The greatest failure of choral groups seems to be the inability to render the emotion rightly. Without true feeling there will be monotony. Feeling gives life, energy, variety, and interest. The symbol that conveys the feeling to the listener is called the emotional tone. Listening outside a room we hear voices, and though we cannot distinguish the words we know the feelings of the speakers; they may be angry or happy, fearful or confident. This is transmitted in their emotional tone. We may listen to a great singing artist interpreting in a language we do not understand, but we are moved by the singing because we feel the emotional tone. If it is in a language we do understand, we should sense both the thought and the feeling.

The best way to lead choristers into the correct interpretation of a choral number is to show them its relationship to the experiences of everyday life. The true feeling of the words must be made apparent to them by tying up the words to a story, a thought-picture, or a common phrase out of their daily experiences. With the added help of well-written music, this should project both the thought and the feeling. Intelligent preparation is necessary for the director, and practice is necessary for the choir if interpretation is to be sincere.

The thought of the words " Come, let us tune our loft-

iest song, and raise to Christ our joyful strain " is a calling
for a joint expression of worship and praise. But what is
the mood, or what emotional tone should be used? Should
these words be rendered as a command, with a lackadaisical attitude, as a despairing plea? Should they be exploded,
wailed, soliloquized, panted, spluttered, growled, stam-
mered, whispered, decreed, teased, yawned, moaned,
whined? There are countless emotional tones that might
be used in uttering every phrase of every song. The director must choose the one that he thinks most closely represents the true feeling. His next task is to find a common
phrase that every one has used and can feel. If he decides
it should be sung with the feeling of a joyful invitation to
help in a worth-while project, the director might suggest
the following phrase, " Come, John, let's go together to
thank him." The choir should be asked to say it spon-
taneously, freely, with no thought of how they are saying
it but with all thought on meaning what they are saying.
Then the original phrase should be said with the same
spontaneity and abandon. This process should be repeated
until the two phrases have the same emotional tone. Trans-
ferring this to singing will offer little problem.

MORE THOUGHTS ON INTERPRETATION

A few years ago an out-of-town orchestra played in New
York. Virgil Thomson, critic of the *New York Herald
Tribune,* wrote an apathetic review and concluded with
this arresting statement: " In music-making, it is always
better to be wrong than reserved."

Here is an outstanding music critic telling us that anything is better than a cold, indifferent, lackadaisical rendition of music. Music is life interpreted in a tonal art, and

" Life is real! Life is earnest! " No one is interested in life that goes along its monotonous little way, monotonous and little because the one living it has no will and incentive to make it otherwise. If one is living that kind of life, he should not call others' attention to it and should not force his living on others. Life should be lived to the full — valiantly, nobly! And music that interprets life should be so rendered — expressively, colorfully!

Are we reading too much into Mr. Thomson's sentence? I think not, and I think music makers could profitably reflect long upon his words.

What does this mean to the church musician? Honestly now, how much of the music heard in the church really expresses any phase of life, how much of it is really satisfying, from an interpretive point of view? Little, if any, would have to be the answer of honesty. Some may say, " Church music has a different reason for existing than concert music." To which I reply that church music was conceived to express the spiritual phases of life, while concert music expresses the more secular phases.

Music, sacred or secular, should interpret moods and emotions. Most church music fails miserably of its intended end. Can we lay the blame at the studio of the composer? No; there is much music effectively written. We, so-called interpreters, must take the blame and strive to find a way to give meaning to the music we use.

To become an artist one must develop a fluent technique with the means he is going to use for expression, and he must learn to project both the thought and the emotional feeling of the work he chooses to interpret.

The choirmaster must make the instrument he is going to use before he can develop a " fluent technique." Voices must be found and brought out, a balance of parts must be provided, musicianship of at least a fair grade must be taught. Then the conductor must make the choristers into a flexible unit that sings with good tone quality, diction, intonation, vitality, and so on. How many choirs are brought this far along? But this is still in the technique of producing tone and is not in the field of interpretation. As commendable as is good technique, you can still have it and, as Virgil Thomson says, be " reserved," that is, not give music life or meaning.

May we take Rev. 3:15-16 out of its setting and have it apply here?

" I know your works: you are neither cold nor hot. Would that you were cold or hot! So, because you are luke-warm, and neither cold nor hot, I will spew you out of my mouth."

A choir that has only tonal technique is lukewarm.

Why is it difficult for the average singers to express with any emotional color the words they are called upon to sing? Because the words generally are not part of their day-by-day living, either in thought or in action. Let any one of our singers have positive convictions about the morals of our generation, or the fairness of a business transaction, or the virtues of a certain political party, and he will speak with emotional color and emphasis. Or again, let him really be in love and speak endearingly to the beloved, or sud-denly come upon a beautiful panorama of nature, or be overwhelmed by a vast cathedral or an appealing painting, then the exclamation will carry sincerity, earnestness, and conviction. These experiences and feelings are parts of his life. The classical, Biblical, and poetic phrases that are sung must be tied up to the day-by-day experiences of life that have the same feeling, although secular.

This is not the ultimate in interpretation or all that the

conductor needs to consider, but if this plan is carried out, it will give color and naturalness to singing. The making effective of this method of interpretation rests solely upon the director, his care in study, and his selection of the right mood and common phrase.[19]

The director through empathy can do much to control the posture, breathing, tone intensity, phrase line, phonetics, interpretation, and emotional tone of the choir. His physical presence, his hands, and his facial expressions can convey his desires to the choristers. If the choir is sensitive and willing, the director, through the power of his personality and leadership, can exert a kind of energizing influence over his choristers which will bring them to the point where they will project the thought and the feeling of the words and music of great sacred writings to the eternal blessing of congregation and choir alike.

THE REHEARSAL — THE CHORAL HEART

What the heart is to the human system the rehearsal is to the life, activity, and growth of a choir. A weak or diseased heart impairs or destroys the human body; similarly, poorly planned and conducted rehearsals impair or destroy the choral body.

Let us notice the parallels between the diseases of the human heart and those of the choral heart.

There are two general classifications of heart ailments, organic and functional. The inadequacies of the various parts of the heart lead to what doctors call organic diseases, in contradistinction to functional diseases, which are outside ailments affecting an otherwise sound organ.

If a director has in his choir voices that are too old or too worn out, persons whose pitch or rhythmic sense is by nature very poor, persons whose health is not good, or persons with quick tempers or bad dispositions, he is bound to find that he has organic heart trouble to contend with. When a child is born with a leaky valve in his heart, we know his whole life will be affected by it; it will retard the functioning of every member of his body. He will never have the vitality that would otherwise be his. If the director has in his choir any of the above-mentioned "leaky valves," he will find the life and effectiveness of his choir greatly retarded.

Suppose we have an organically sound choral heart to work with. There are still many functional diseases that may attack it and in time destroy it.

In the heart there is a set of nerves called the "pacemaker." When the pacemaker is upset and the person has, technically speaking, a bundle branch block, the rhythm of the heart is unsteady. The heart must function in a regular rhythm to perform at maximum efficiency. What this nerve-center pacemaker is to the human heart, the director is to the choral heart. The director sets the rhythm of the choir. If he is casual in his approach to the rehearsal, the choir will be the same; if he is unprepared, the choir will get little from the rehearsal; if he is slovenly about his appearance, his posture, his conduct, he can expect the same from his group; if he is flippant and irreligious about the performance of sacred music, he will get the same attitude from the choir. On the other hand, if he comes to the rehearsal on time, thoroughly prepared, careful about his person, with a love of God and a desire to help his choir prepare for the musical leadership responsibilities of the Sabbath, he will set the rhythm for the choral heart and keep it beating steadily and effectively. The director is the pacemaker.

If a muscle of the heart fails to develop and is not strong enough to carry its share of the burden, we have, in doctors' parlance, myocardial failure. He can easily liken this to the failure of an individual or a section of the choir to carry its share of the choral load. Nowhere is teamwork more necessary than in a vocal ensemble. J. Mason Knox said it was

" the everlastin' teamwork
Of every bloomin' soul " [20]

that made for success. In a choir where one section or even
one individual is not doing his best for the ensemble as a
whole, we have choral myocardial failure. Each section of
the choir should be trained to have the best possible unison tone, then to so merge that tone with the others that
a homogeneous effect will be produced. This is an ideal,
of course, but it is a goal to which every individual must
willingly work, with the director showing the way.

If the heart has to cope with weak, anemic blood or
wrong blood pressure, its functions are impaired. High or
low blood pressure is equally detrimental. Music that is
too hard or that is too easy is bad for the choir. A choir
with average intelligence and musicianship can sing almost
anything that is within the ability of the director to teach.
Obviously the average choir should not attempt choruses
from the Bach *B Minor Mass,* for instance, but the vast
majority of choral literature is well within the abilities of
the choir if it is within the intellectual and musical capaci-
ties of the director. However, music that is too difficult will
give a choir " high blood pressure."

Low blood pressure is an equally lamentable functional
disorder. Music that is too easy is sometimes found in the
rehearsal room. I would not have you put a premium on
difficult music as such, but I do urge you to use music that
will challenge the interest, musicianship, and spirituality
of the choir members.

If a person lives on a monotonous diet, the quality of
the blood may be impaired and a blood deficiency result
which disturbs the normal working of the heart. The rehearsals must be varied. Human beings, especially those

with any artistic impulses, rebel at monotony. If the choir member knows the next rehearsal is going to be the same as the last one, he has little incentive for regularity in attendance. Make each rehearsal different; always make your choristers expectant. They should never be quite sure how this new anthem will be presented, how that new vocal problem will be solved, what new idea will be brought into rehearsal to make it interesting. The director should not in any sense be trying to put on a show or entertainment, but he must carry on his teaching with the principle of variety in presentation.

The adult choir will need one or, on occasion, two full evenings a week to rehearse. The rehearsal should be two hours in length, with a short break at about the midway point. The night of the week seems to make little difference. A twenty- or thirty-minute warm-up and rehearsal should be held before each service.

The Rehearsal Room

The room to be used for rehearsals is an important consideration. Unfortunately, many churches made little or no provision for adequate choir rehearsal rooms when their physical structures were erected. The architects and church fathers seemed to say, in effect, " Any room will have to do to practice in." But any room will not do. It is unlikely that any really beautiful choral tone or religious interpretation could be developed in a room poorly ventilated, poorly lighted, barren, dingy, unattractive, and with poor acoustical properties. Yet many choirs are forced to rehearse in just such uninspiring, unartistic surroundings. Someone may say, " Why not rehearse in the auditorium? " Aside from the winter heating cost, singing in an empty auditorium presents difficult acoustical problems. If the churchmen want the choirs to do good singing, they should provide a good rehearsal room.

The ideal room must be well ventilated. The lights must be rather bright and in such a position that the singers do not face them. The room should be about square with a high ceiling; an arched or domed ceiling is best. The room should be large enough to give the singers a feeling of freedom and large enough to allow the voices to sound normal. A choir of fifty should have a rehearsal room that would comfortably seat three or four times that number.

A choir should not rehearse in a long, narrow room. No matter which way the singers face in such a room the acoustical problems are extremely disturbing. If the singers face the end of the room, echoes will cause trouble; if the sides, the tone will become strident because of the rebound of sound from the close wall.

The seats in the rehearsal room should be arranged as they are in the choir loft. It is best to rehearse in the same position as that from which they will sing. If the choir loft has various levels for the rows, it is a decided advantage to have the rehearsal room arranged the same.

The rehearsal room, as one of its essentials, must have a good piano, kept in accurate tune. The room must be kept clean and neat. A blackboard should be available. A bulletin board placed near the door may be used for announcements, programs, instructions, and so on. The room should be made simply attractive, a pleasant place in which to assemble and strive for spiritual and artistic results.

SEATING POSITION

The best seating position for a choir is something each director will have to determine for his own group. He is, of course, restricted in his arrangement by the size and shape of his choir loft. There are several things about the structure of choral music that should be considered in seating the various parts:

1. In homophonic music, which forms a large part of the anthem repertoire of Protestant churches, there is a melody (usually in the soprano part) supported by harmony in the other voices. The entire harmonic structure is based upon the lowest or bass part. This part forms the foundation upon which the other parts build the chord. It is very necessary that this lowest part be seated so that it may be distinctly heard by all other parts.

2. The outer parts of the chord, soprano and bass, generally move together or form the most common intervals of the harmony, i.e., octaves, fifths, or thirds. These parts should be seated near one another where they can tune easily. Just as a piano tuner tests with these intervals, so the outer voices must tune one to another.

3. The inner voices, altos and tenors, often move at the same time and in consonant intervals, so that they should approximate one another.

4. In eight-part singing it is advantageous to have the outer voices (first tenors and second basses, first sopranos and second altos, first sopranos and second basses, first tenors and second altos) near each other for harmonic tuning.

In the light of these four points, the following choir seating positions are recommended:

For a four-part choir —

Tenor		Bass	
Alto		Soprano	

For an eight-part choir —

2d Tenor	1st Tenor	2d Bass	1st Bass
1st Alto	2d Alto	1st Soprano	2d Soprano

The Director's Preparation

The director has much study to do before a new anthem is presented to the choir in rehearsal. He must be completely familiar with each part, he should spot the measures most likely to give difficulty, he must decide on the desired emotional tone and how to obtain it. He must study the anthem for its musical form and style. He should know about the composer and author. He must consider the anthem for its effect in the service. Many of these points he will want to talk over with the choir in the course of the preparation of the anthem. If the director has complete mastery of the number, he can teach it in a relatively short time. However, plenty of time for rehearsal should be allowed for every anthem. The director should plan the rehearsal to include work on anthems for several Sundays in advance.

Plan the rehearsal. Many directors fail to accomplish as much as they should in each rehearsal because they do not organize the practice period.

Plan the rehearsal as to time. Not only start and end on time, but plan the amount of time you want to spend on each part of the rehearsal.

Plan the rehearsal as to the order of material to be studied. Build your rehearsal program as a concert performer builds his program. That is, if possible, do not use two anthems in succession that are in the same key or even in the same mode. Do not use two chorale-type anthems or two polyphonic numbers in succession. Build your rehearsal order for contrast and climax.

Pick out the most necessary points to study in each anthem, and concentrate on different points in different anthems. In one you may pay particular attention to rhythm; in another, to the unusual intervals, blend of voices, intonation, phonetics, projection of the mood, and so on. Plan what you want to accomplish in each rehearsal with each anthem.

Plan the rehearsal as to relaxation. Two hours is too long to sit in a rehearsal without some moving about. The last third of the rehearsal period will yield better results if there has been an opportunity for physical activity. This may be accomplished by five minutes of setting-up exercises, processional practice, or a recess period.

Plan the rehearsal as to unusual things that will be of value and interest.

Rehearsals may wisely include some sight reading. Read new hymns. After the sections are familiar with their own parts, turn them around, i.e., sopranos read bass, for example.

Rounds may be used advantageously to give a feeling of part independence. Don't use the old, worn-out ones. Teach new ones.

Have some of the solos in anthems sung in unison by the entire section. This gives them an opportunity to work for complete blend of voices.

Time can often be saved in the learning of involved anthems if the various sections of the choir can work in different rooms at the same time. Generally there are some choir members who can help the director in these sectional rehearsals.

Teach as much voice culture and musicianship as possible during rehearsals. The choir members should, after a year in a chorus, be much better singers and musicians than before, but they must be taught in small, regular, interesting doses which they will enjoy assimilating.

In most cities there are now facilities for having record-

ings made of your choir. The cost is not high, but the value
to the director is great. The choir will be keenly interested in this, and it gives the director opportunity to point
out the good and bad qualities in their singing.

The life and growth of a choral group is not in its public
performances, but in its rehearsals. The choir will rise
directly in proportion to the amount of thought, energy,
musicianship, and spiritual value a director puts into each
rehearsal. It will start to fall as soon as the director begins
to come to rehearsals unprepared. Fine choral groups are
made by fine rehearsals.

INTONATION

With the greatly increased use of *a cappella* music by
the average church choir in the last few decades, the director finds he is forced to give much thought as to how to
maintain accurate intonation. He may have noted slight
deviations in pitch in accompanied anthems, but the organ
would always pull them back without serious results. An
unaccompanied anthem, however, presents a much greater
problem. If a choir has all the other characteristics of a
good choral group and fails in this one point, intonation,
it is immediately classed as a poor chorus. The effect of
losing pitch is demoralizing to the singers; upon the congregation, whether they are conscious of its cause or not,
the effect is discomfiture.

Among the common causes of faulty intonation the
director will find: [21] a stuffy room, physical or mental
fatigue, nervousness, poorly trained voices, carelessness in
singing intervals, poor acoustical surroundings. The director will see to it that all these adverse conditions are
eliminated just as far as possible. But suppose the choir

still goes flat! (Sharping is rare; it is generally due to over-anxiety and nervousness.) Warnings, exhortations, special vocalizings all bring no results! Are we to believe that the choir cannot sing *a cappella?* Many directors have come up to this point and have been extremely distraught.

There is one fact that has been overlooked. The key of the composition must be just the right key for the choir. Some time ago there appeared an article by William Ripley Dorr, entitled " The Influence of Pitch Upon Intonation," [22] which included the following enlightening observations:

" Many years ago I learned that it frequently happens that it is impossible for a choir to keep the pitch when singing a number in the original key, but that they will keep the pitch perfectly when it is transposed even so little as a semitone higher. Occasionally it is necessary to put it up as much as a major third before the effect is right and the intonation is perfect.

" In our repertory we have many *a cappella* anthems, ranging from simple things like Farrant's ' Lord, for Thy Tender Mercies' Sake,' which is written in F and goes best in A flat, to some of the fine Russian things, and with one solitary exception, we have found it necessary to raise the pitch from a semitone to a major third, for satisfactory *a cappella* performance. This one exception is Farrant's ' Call to Remembrance,' and here the publishers, Curwen, raised the pitch for us. My copy of the *Musical Times* edition is in D minor; Curwen has raised this to F minor, where with us it stays beautifully.

" Thus it is safe to generalize that when a choir knows the notes perfectly, but slips off pitch in a particular number, it may help matters to try the number in a higher key. Incidentally, this device is as effective with our mixed choir as it is with the boys and men. And it is effective not only with *a cappella* music but also with accompanied anthems.

" Why this should be, I do not even pretend to know. It may be that the greater tension of vocal cords caused by the higher pitch inspires greater effort on the singer's part, which results in more perfect singing of the intervals and consequently in better intonation. This is mere speculation. As far as I can see there is no way we can ever be sure we have the correct explanation of this strange situation, but as long as we are masters of it, we may well be content."

Noble Cain in his book *Choral Music and Its Practice* seems to corroborate Mr. Dorr's finding when he refers to " the worn musical groove " as being one cause of flatting.

It may be found that a key that is right for a choir one year may not be right for it the next year. Mr. Dorr, in the article referred to, tells of his experience with the " Dresden Amen." The key of A was right for his boys one year, but the following year it was necessary to pitch it in B flat before accurate intonation could be maintained.

The writer has found that, though it is often necessary to raise the pitch for a successful *a cappella* performance, in some anthems it is necessary to lower it. The right pitch for the choir is not always above the one in which it is printed. Whether a composition is in sharps or flats seems to make no difference to the choir, but the right key is important.

This device of changing the pitch is not a substitute for careful preparation of all the musical detail, nor should it be employed until all other possible causes of pitch deviation have been eliminated. It will, however, often solve a confounding problem when everything else has failed.

REPERTOIRE FOR ADULT CHOIRS

An important responsibility of the director is the selection of anthems. This is a most influential part of his work. He is called upon to select music through which the congregation will endeavor to worship God. He must choose anthems that will challenge the singers to do their best, but they must not be so difficult that the singers will be discouraged by them. A director's musical training, his general education, his religious convictions, and to some extent his character will be revealed in the music he selects for his choirs.

No one would dare set down dogmatic rules for the selection of effective anthems for all churches and all choirs. Certain guideposts may be suggested, however, that will help the director in this vital part of his work.

WORDS

The words should fit the intellectual level and understanding of the people who sing them and of the people who worship through them. "Thou All-transcendent Deity," by Palestrina (E. C. Schirmer, Inc.), is an excellent worship anthem for some churches, but in others it would not be clearly understood, and a congregation would have difficulty in worshiping through it. We should in no way " sing down " to a congregation or choir, but their comprehension should be considered.

If the words are in poetic form, they should be good poetry. Doggerel should never be used in the worship of God.

The words should be impersonal. Public worship is a group expression. The words should be in a form that is logical for a group utterance. " To thee, O Lord, our hearts we raise " would be more appropriate for an anthem or hymn than " Give ear to my voice, O Lord, when I call upon thee." In private worship the individual communes; in public worship we voice common emotions.

The best words for worship music are Scriptural in sentiment, expression, or phraseology. It is not enough that they should not violate Scriptural truths; the very form in which the thought is cast must be true to Holy Writ. Although words taken from the Scriptures or Scriptural paraphrases are not prerequisites of good anthems, it will be noted that most of the best worship materials are taken from this source.

MUSIC

The music should be free from secular association. The concert stage, the opera house, and the theater must not be brought into the church. Despite the apparently obvious fact that music intended for secular use would not be usable in a church worship service, some congregations are invited to worship through the music of " A Perfect Day " (Bond), " Calm as the Night " (Bohm), or " Andante Cantabile " (Tschaikowsky), and so on. Just be-

cause so-called sacred words have been put to a tune, it
does not therefore become fit worship material. The use
of the words " Come, Gracious Spirit, Heavenly Dove "
does not make a good anthem out of Franz's " Dedication."

To the concertgoer or the voice student it is still a secular
song. The words " O Lord on High, We Pray Thee, Guide
Us " do not make of Mozart's *Magic Flute* aria a good
worship service solo. One could cite examples ad infinitum.
Adaptations of melodies from ancient works that have entirely lost their secular connection may be used. Many of
the dignified chorales were once associated with secular
words.

The best worship music is free from secular idioms.
Joseph W. Clokey states this admirably when he writes:

" If the melody is sweet, suave, obvious, chromatic, or sequential, it will be unfit — these are the devices of the popular ballad. If the rhythm employs many dotted notes, triplets, syncopation, rhythmic sequences, it is unfit — these are the devices of the dance music. If the harmony makes use of chromatic chords, modern dissonances, successive dominant seventh chords, diminished chords, it is unfit — these are the devices of the modern concert-room harmony." [23]

Remember that the object of music in the church is to direct the attention of the listener toward God; you are not entertaining or displaying your skill.

The music should not be too long. If the music is used to intensify the religious emotion of the portion of the service in which it is found, it is best that it be brief and forceful, increasing that emotion and then stopping. In the first *Concord Anthem Book* (E. C. Schirmer, Inc.), eighteen of the forty anthems are three pages in length or less, and nine more are but four pages in length. Bach chorales or just one part of a longer anthem are often completely adequate.

Just as the words should be impersonal, so should the music. An anthem or solo that projects the personality of the singer, the very thing a soloist is trying to develop in secular music, is not the best worship material.

Worship anthems should be simple. It is encouraging to those with limited choral resources to realize, and it should be thought about by all directors, that the best worship anthems are simple, not ornate and elaborate. It is generally acknowledged that the highest art forms are the simplest. " It is well known that it is far more difficult to write good music that is simple than that which is difficult, and the truest artistry is often shown not in prodigality of resources, but in economy of material and effective use of limited resources." [24]

WORDS AND MUSIC

The words and music must agree, not only as to rhythm and accent, but in another way that composers have so often forgotten. The thought content of a word passage as a whole should be the guide to the composer when writing music for that passage. Often composers have let the mood suggested by a few words, considered alone, govern the type of music for a section. For instance, the thought of the following passage as a whole is confidence and faith in our Good Shepherd:

" Yea, though I walk through the valley of the shadow of
     death,
  I will fear no evil: for thou art with me;
  Thy rod and thy staff they comfort me."

                                                  Ps. 23:4

How many composers have given music to this entire passage expressing confidence and faith? They have taken the words, " Yea, though I walk through the valley of the shadow of death," and written gloomy, minor music for it. They show a sudden change of mood when the words " I will fear no evil " are reached. This is absurd, yet all composers, from Schubert to the least of them, have done it when setting the Twenty-third Psalm. The mood of the music must mirror the mood of the words as a whole.

The anthem may meet the strictest requirements and be perfectly suited for use in a worship service, but it may still fall short of its full usefulness if it is used in an inappropriate part of the service. An anthem of humility will miss the mark if used in the adoration part of the service. An anthem of consecration, used before the worshiper is prepared for it, will likewise fail.

To select anthems that will lead men in their communion with their Creator is no task to be taken lightly.[25]

Consider All the Flock

In an effort to be a true minister of music to all the people, the director should feel that it is sound occasionally to use anthems that feed "such as have need of milk, and not of strong meat" (Heb. 5:12-14). In most congregations there are those "unskilful in the word of righteousness" who need a simple musical diet. These must be nurtured until they can assimilate the "strong meat" which "belongeth to them that are of full age."

There are those who will be more helped by " My God and I " (Sergei) than by " Here Yet a While " from *The St. Matthew Passion* (Bach). In the selection of anthems, the " My God and I " people should not be ignored; neither should the director feel that everyone is helped by the more subtle, mystical anthems that may feed his soul.

A study of the congregation should be made and consideration given to all degrees of spiritual maturity. Anthems should be selected that will help all the people to "worship the Lord" and to "grow in grace."

If directors will but heed the suggestions of the preceding paragraphs, there will be fewer failures on the choir-loft podium and more happiness on the part of both congregation and choir, not incidentally, more worshipers finding the music of their church helpful in their spiritual growth.

If this seems like " fence-straddling," we have good company, for did not Paul say, " I have become all things to all men, that I might by all means save some " (I Cor. 9:22)?

OCCASIONAL CHOIRS

If the director of music and the choir system is to minister to the entire congregation, and if the music of the church is to give an opportunity to everyone who wishes to do so to participate, account must be taken of other groups. Those " graduated " from the adult choir, those who are so employed that they cannot give the necessary time to the regular rehearsals of a permanent choir, and those whose musical talents are meager but who still have a desire for musical utterance must be given a place. To serve these people the director will plan for special groups for various occasions. Such occasional choirs give opportunity for all those who have any musical urge to share in the exhilarating experience of group expression. No tryouts are held for any of these choirs.

MALE CHORUS

Everyone enjoys a male chorus. With the men of the adult choir and the young people's choir as a backbone, it is entirely possible to have a male chorus that will sing creditably once or twice a year.

If there is a men's class in the church school, work from that group. Get the co-operation of the class officers, explain the plan (it should not be necessary to have more than one or two rehearsals before the singing) , and ask for volunteers. If there is no men's class, make personal contacts with likely prospects. Spot the men of the congregation who sing in the church service, get a list of prospects from the pastor and music committee. Some of the extra men may be able to sing parts, but most of them will do best on the melody. Call the rehearsal for a time that is convenient for the men, have simple but good male chorus music ready, seat your adult choir men in advantageous places to help the rest, conduct your rehearsal in business-like manner, and everyone will be surprised at what a fine male chorus has been developed.

This chorus should be assembled for a distinct program or service. The men may sing in a special men's service in church, at a Father's Day service, at a father-and-son dinner, and so on. A choir entirely composed of fathers and their sons will be of interest.

Music for such a group may be regular male chorus music in which the unchanged voices will sing the melody in their soprano octave, doubling the male chorus melody. If the boys are particularly good singers, regular mixed-voice music may be used, the boys singing the soprano and alto, the men the tenor and bass. Such a choir will greatly interest the boys and be of value in bringing the fathers closer to the church and the choir program.

LADIES' CHORUS

An occasional ladies' chorus is also of value and interest. The director may work through the women's society or women's church school class to enlist recruits for this choir. The procedure should be much like that suggested for the men. Be sure of plenty of altos; most ladies' choruses have too few. Music written for ladies' two- or three-part chorus may be used. An appropriate time for this choir to sing is on Mother's Day or at some general women's meeting. A mother-and-daughter choir may also be developed for some particular occasion.

ORATORIO CHORUS

Once a year all those who wish to sing should be invited to join in the preparation and presentation of some large choral work. These may include those who have formerly been members of the adult choir, all the extra singers who have helped in the occasional male chorus or ladies' chorus, the adult choir, the older members of the young people's choir, and any others who desire to take part.

The Christmas portion of *The Messiah* (Handel) is ideal for such an oratorio chorus. Many people at some time have sung parts of this oratorio and are delighted to have an opportunity to sing it again. With the adult choir preparing the more difficult passages ahead of the first joint rehearsal, a good performance can be developed in three or four rehearsals. Do not try to use all the choruses the first year, but make this oratorio rendition an annual event, increasing the number of choruses each season. *The Creation* (Haydn), *Elijah* (Mendelssohn), *Crucifixion* (Stainer), *The Seven Last Words* (Dubois), and so on, all may be effectively sung by an oratorio chorus of this kind.

THE CONGREGATION AS A CHOIR

The ultimate goal of a graded choir plan is a congregation that can understand, appreciate, worship through, and even participate in the choral music of the church. This congregational participation in anthems is not new in some churches, notably the Scotch, Welsh, and Cornish churches. In the American Protestant Church, however, it is all but unheard of. It will not be so uncommon in the future if the church continues to embrace the multiple-choir plan. It has been a custom at oratorio chorus *Messiah* performances at the writer's church to distribute copies of the " Hallelujah Chorus " to the audience with the request that they join in this number. The result is so stimulating and inspiring that this will doubtless continue to be a feature of the annual performance. Also the congregation joins the choirs in singing the refrain of " The Palms " (Fauré) each Palm Sunday. In recent years several publishers have brought out hymn-anthems in which the congregation is expected to sing on a final stanza.

Choir of Families

Recreationists say, " Families that play together stay together." Let the minister of music say, " Families that sing together cling together."

Make an occasion, at least once a year, when a choir of families will fill the choir loft. The pastor and the people will be thrilled to see dads and mothers with Johnnys, Marys, and white-haired grandmas too, file in, sit as families, and lead in a service. An appropriate time for this is on the Sunday that honors the Christian home, often observed simultaneously with Mother's Day.

It matters little if Dad can't carry his part and fakes a bass, or if Mother's voice wobbles badly. What matters is that families are joining in serving and worshiping. A half-hour rehearsal before service is generally sufficient to acquaint these choristers with details and to rehearse their parts of a hymn or simple song to be sung as a " special." It is best not to use vestments and to keep the service and the families' participation as simple as possible.

In the church the writer is serving, a choir of families is used annually in an informal Christmas morning service. The plan has been to ask families to participate who have some children in the choirs. When the director feels that the song to be used needs a little extra rehearsing, a copy is sent to each home for family practicing. The singers are urged to wear a new Christmas tie or blouse, and the children are asked to bring a new toy or Christmas doll. Of course these are taken right into the choir loft. Frivolous, you say? But very heart-warming as we celebrate the birth of the One who came as a child and blessed the family.

Summer Choir

Summertime for most people means weekends away and vacations, a relaxing from the routines of the winter season, a " let's take it easier " attitude. These are on the debit side as far as choirs are concerned. But let us look on the credit side. In summer some people find their occupations not so demanding; there are some young folks home from college; and in many communities there are vacation visitors or summer school students. The wise director will strive to balance these factors and plan for a summer choir that will effectively " carry on."

Here is a plan that has worked. Expect your adult choir members to sing at least half of the ten to twelve Sundays designated as summer Sundays. Expect your high school choir members to sing in the summer choir at least half of the summer Sundays. In May write all members of the church who have been away in college (especially those who have been in the choirs) , requesting them to serve their church in a singing capacity at least part of the time during their vacations. Cast a dragnet throughout the parish for those who may have more leisure time in July and August. " Now it is your turn. Sing and serve in the summer choir." This can be the slogan. Contact the schools in the vicinity that may have visiting summer school students. Welcome singers who can join even for a few weeks. Give special invitations to the new families in the church and to those who have had some " feel" for the music programs by having taken part in the other " occasional choruses."

Plan your summer music to have many attractive features. This will interest the singers and the congregation and will magnify the singing of the summer choir and give it more purpose.

These subjects have been used as themes for the summer music on various Sundays in the last few years in the writer's church. In some instances, only the anthems followed the theme; in others, the organ numbers and congregational hymns reinforced the subject.

Folk Songs of the Southern Mountains, arrangements by John Jacob Niles. G. Schirmer, Inc.

Music by the American Moravians, arrangements by Clarence Dickinson. The H. W. Gray Company, Inc.

Hymns of the American Frontier, arranged for mixed voices by Robert G. McCutchan. G. Schirmer, Inc.

Anthems with Violin Obbligatos
Some of the anthems used were:

Bach-Holler, " Jesu, Joy of Man's Desiring." The H. W. Gray Company, Inc.

Gluck-Riegger, " O Saviour, Hear Me." Harold Flammer, Inc.

Franck, " O Lord Most Holy." G. Schirmer, Inc.

Bizet-Ryder, " Lamb of God." Theodore Presser Co.

Yon, " The Infant Jesus." J. Fischer & Bro.

Christmas in July

All Christmas music, a yearly feature.

New Hymns Used as Anthems

Obtained from The Hymn Society of America, 297 Fourth Avenue, New York 10, N. Y.

Fourth of July Sunday Cantata

H. Alexander Matthews, " Recessional " (Kipling). G. Schirmer, Inc. Brass quartet parts available.

Anthems with Antiphonal Effects

Palestrina, " Alleluia, Lord God." E. C. Schirmer, Inc.

Luther-Dickinson, " Sanctus." The H. W. Gray Company, Inc.

Dickinson, "List to the Lark." The H. W. Gray Company, Inc.

Bitgood, " Hosanna." The H. W. Gray Company, Inc.

Pfohl, " Hosanna." Brodt Music Company.

Bach, " At Thy Feet." B. F. Wood Co.

Negro Spirituals

Music of One Particular Nationality

Such as English, Russian, Italian, French, German.

Music by One Particular Composer

Such as Mozart, Bach, Schubert, Clokey, Dickinson, Carl F. Mueller.

Choruses, Solos, and Episodes from Oratorios and Cantatas

Such as *Elijah* (Mendelssohn) ; *The Creation* (Haydn) ; "Hear My Prayer" (Mendelssohn) ; *Gallia* (Gounod).

God as Revealed in Nature

Anthems used were:

Elgar, " As Torrents in Summer." The H. W. Gray Company, Inc.

Beethoven, " The Heavens Are Telling." E. C. Schirmer, Inc.

Schubert, " The Omnipotence." G. Schirmer, Inc.

Rogers, " Seek Him That Maketh the Seven Stars." Theodore Presser Co.

Nagler-Dickinson, " A Song in Praise of the Lord of Heaven and Earth." The H. W. Gray Company, Inc.

Anthems Based on Familiar Hymns

Anthems used were:

Davidson, "Ye Watchers and Ye Holy Ones." E. C. Schirmer, Inc.

Thiman, " Immortal, Invisible." The H. W. Gray Company, Inc.

Mueller, " Now Thank We All Our God." G. Schirmer, Inc.

Ward, " All Hail the Power of Jesus' Name." Harold Flammer, Inc. Brass parts available.

Ringwald, various hymn arrangements. Shawnee Press, Inc.

Luther-Olds, " A Mighty Fortress." Hall and McCreary Co.
William-Shaw, " For All the Saints." G. Schirmer, Inc.
Wilson, " Jesus, Lover of My Soul." Lorenz Co. Tune, " Refuge."

Obviously most of these subjects could be effectively used during the regular choir season when a stimulating idea is desired.

VERSE-SPEAKING CHOIR

Another choir that the director may develop is a verse-speaking choir. This may be an occasional choir or perhaps a permanent choir. In most churches the Scripture and Psalter readings are unimpressively done. They are read in a singsong fashion with little expression, meaning, or significance. This part of the service has in many churches deteriorated into a perfunctory utterance. A verse-speaking choir may be of value as a method of arousing interest in the reading of the Scriptures.

Stir some high-school-age group with the possibilities of the choric speaking of a Bible passage. Train it in the intelligent reading and interpreting of a psalm, then use it in a young people's meeting or a regular church service. It may well be that such a group will bring a new interest in the reading of Holy Writ, and it may lead to the organization of a permanent speaking choir.[26]

The occasional use of choric speaking with one or more of the regular choirs is recommended for developing good diction, for creating a new interest in poetry and prose, for teaching certain great religious utterances, and for adding variety to the work of the choirs.

INSTRUMENTAL GROUPS

If one is to minister to the whole church, he must not be unmindful of those whose musical interests are instrumental. They should be given an opportunity to serve.

In most churches there are some string players who would like to be called upon occasionally to assist the choirs. Their effective participation will add variety and interest to the music of a service. If there are sufficient players for a "vested string choir," they can provide an impressive accompaniment for an anthem sung by children or adults. Also, they may be heard with benefit in worship music arranged for strings alone.[27]

May a word of admonition be injected here? Unskilled singers under skilled direction may sound well, but unskilled instrumentalists under any kind of direction still sound unskilled. A wrong tone sung does not seem to offend as badly as a wrong note played. The admonition is to be sure the instrumentalists play in tune and in time, with sufficient technique, before asking them to play in public.

What has been said regarding string players also applies to brass players. Use them in services occasionally. There are several times a year when the triumphant tones of the trumpet add the right touch to the spirit of the day. Such times might be Easter, the church anniversary, a patriotic occasion, Thanksgiving, or a church-wide campaign. Some suggested anthems with parts for brass choir are:

Wild, "Blow, Golden Trumpet." The H. W. Gray Company, Inc.

Ward, "All Hail the Power of Jesus' Name." Harold Flammer, Inc.

Matthews, "Recessional" (short cantata). G. Schirmer, Inc.

Olds, " How Brightly Shines the Morning Star." Carl Fischer, Inc.

——, " Sunrise on Easter Morning." Carl Fischer, Inc.

Overley, " That Joyous Easter Day." C. C. Birchard and Company.

Because of the interest created and the musical value resulting, directors are wise to make some use of single instruments with voices. Some suggested anthems in this category for violin and voices are listed under summer choir special features. Other anthems that might be considered are:

Marshall, " None Other Lamb." Carl Fischer, Inc. Cello.

Couper, " The Flute Carol." J. Fischer & Bro. Flute. Flute part readily played from the accompaniment.

Kettring, " God Watches Over All the World." The H. W. Gray Company, Inc. Flute. Flute part readily played from the accompaniment.

Norden, " Charity " (short cantata). The H. W. Gray Company, Inc. Violin and harp.

Also see the extensive catalogue of music arranged by Clarence Dickinson for various instruments and voices. (The H. W. Gray Company, Inc.)

The enterprising director will find an instrumentalist in his church or city who has a flair for composing or arranging and will request his help in writing parts for the available solo instruments to perform with his choirs.

In some churches the director of music may find sufficient material for an orchestra. If he has had instruction along orchestral lines, this would be a worth-while enterprise for him. It might be advisable, however, to turn over this project to a trained instrumental conductor. It is difficult to obtain players for a good full orchestra in a church unless it has close connections with a college or conservatory.

Hand Bell Choir

A recent development in this field of instruments as used in the church is the organization of choirs among children and youth to play English hand bells. This has great potential for the minister of music. In England, hand bell playing is a long-established pastime. In America, adult groups of hand bell players have been in existence for some years, particularly in the New England states. However, the use of hand bell choirs as an aid to the children's choir program is a new development. The bells are fairly simple to play; the tone is mellow and appealing and particularly suited to be used with and by children and young people.

Printed information on hand bell procedures is just beginning to appear.[28] Some music is available from publishers. However, most directors will find that they have to make their own arrangements according to the bells they purchase.

PART TWO

MUSIC AND WORSHIP

14

PROTESTANT WORSHIP

When an artist is preparing to paint a picture, he has a vivid mental concept of what he wants the result to be. He knows what he wants the public to see and feel in his finished painting. When a composer is contemplating a composition, he plans what effect he wants produced through the interpretation of his composition. Similarly the church music director should have a clear idea of what should be accomplished through his music and what effect he is trying to produce upon the congregation with each musical number.

What Is Worship?

What are you striving to achieve through your worship music? You must answer this question. Your answer will be reflected in the music you select, the attitude of your singers toward the music and the whole service, the place you use the music in the service, and the effect your music has on the congregation.

It may help to record here some ideas regarding worship that will guide the director in his thought upon this subject.

Swisher, in his book *Music in Worship,* gives a thought-

provoking definition when he writes, " Worship is a com-
mingling of devotion, adoration, reverence, awe, mystery,
and aspiration." [29] Director, how does your music fit into
that type of worship? Mr. Swisher goes on to say that the
purpose of worship is " the profound stirring of the people, to the end that some beneficent change may be
wrought in their natures that will uplift them and make
them desire to live better lives." Director, does your music
help to do this?

If the purpose of public worship is to stir the religious
emotion of man, what means are there at our disposal to
do this? There seem to be five definite means of helping to
this end.

First, there is the church structure itself. A theater type
of auditorium is not conducive to worship, but upon en-
tering a cathedral we instinctively have a desire to be
hushed and commune with God. However, it is rarely
within the power of the music director to change the archi-
tectural design of the building.

Secondly, there is the use of symbols. Except for the selection and use of vestments, this means also is not often
under the control of the director.

The third aid we have in the stirring of man is the order
of service. In liturgical churches this has been established
for us and is practically unalterable; indeed, we would not
alter it if we could. However, in the congregational type
of church the order of service is largely in the hands of
the pastor and the choir director. There are some who
seem to feel that a service can be thrown together at the
last minute. They think that using any anthem, any hymn,
and any Scripture lesson will give a satisfactory effect. We
do not apply this haphazard method to any other action
in life that we want to be successful; why should we think

it will work in the church? The service of public worship that is not carefully, thoughtfully, and prayerfully prepared is bound to be a failure. It behooves the director to study worship and worship forms to guide him in the selection and preparation of worship music. Subsequent paragraphs will discuss this further.

The fourth means is music itself. This is entirely within the province of the musical director. For many people, music transmits more religious meaning than the spoken word. There are some who attend services solely for the religious uplift they receive through the music. If one were to put a stop watch on the time used for the organ, hymns, anthems, responses, and interludes in an average church service, he might be surprised at the number of minutes music is being heard. Music is not secondary; it is at least of equal importance with the other parts of the service.

The fifth means is entirely out of the director's realm; it is the reading of the Scripture and its interpretation in the sermon.

The mind of man responds best to order. A chaotic condition is foreign to his nature. He functions best when there is a system, and he is constantly systematizing his own work to get the best results. Not only is this true in the physical and intellectual realms, but in the spiritual and emotional realms as well. If we are trying to stir the emotions of man through our worship service and we know that he responds best when there is a definite sequence of thought, our responsibility is to find the order of service that has the sequence that will best move him.

As might be expected, the Bible gives us clearly the progression that stirs men to action. The first eight verses of the sixth chapter of Isaiah describe what we might well consider an ideal worship service. The worshiper is led through various steps to the ultimate goal of all worship services, the cry, " Here I am! Send me."

The first experience in Isaiah's worship service may be called " adoration of God." This is described for us in the first four verses:

" In the year that King Uzziah died I saw the Lord sitting upon a throne, high and lifted up; and his train filled the temple. Above him stood the seraphim; each had six wings: with two he covered his face, and with two he covered his feet, and with two he flew. And one called to another and said:
" ' Holy, holy, holy is the Lord of hosts;
the whole earth is full of his glory.'
And the foundations of the thresholds shook at the voice of him who called, and the house was filled with smoke."

The second step we will call " humiliation of self." This is found in the fifth verse:

" And I said: ' Woe is me! For I am lost; for I am a man of unclean lips, and I dwell in the midst of a people of unclean lips; for my eyes have seen the King, the Lord of hosts! ' "

The sixth and seventh verses bring in the element of " purification."

" Then flew one of the seraphim to me, having in his hand a burning coal which he had taken with tongs from the altar. And he touched my mouth, and said: ' Behold, this has touched your lips; your guilt is taken away, and your sin forgiven.' "

The final step, " consecration," is found in the eighth verse:

" And I heard the voice of the Lord saying, ' Whom shall I send, and who will go for us? ' Then I said, ' Here I am! Send me.' "

Let us note a few things about this worship service. Four verses are used to describe the adoration. This is a very important part of the service; it is the first Godward urge that should be felt in the service. Much of this must come through music. If music of humiliation or consecration is used in this early part of the service, it will fail. The congregation must first worship through adoration. Note that the second element, humiliation, came as a result of the adoration (" for my eyes have seen the King, the Lord of hosts! "). There is no reason for humiliation unless there has been a vision of something or Someone better.

Notice that the five definite means of stirring man referred to earlier were all present: the building, symbols, order of service, music, and a well-planned sermon. Note too that the sermon was short. It needed to be no longer, for the heart of the worshiper had been prepared by the preceding steps.

A worship service that is planned in accordance with this adoration-humiliation-purification-consecration formula has the Word of God for its authority and has proved its usefulness.

The writers [30] who have traced for us the history of religious rituals and liturgies have been unanimous in declaring that " the study of our various liturgies shows that all are built on a definite structural plan. There was a true sense of proportion and of climax in the minds of those who conceived them." [31] The liturgy of the Eastern church, the Mass of the Western church, the Anglican Church Prayer Book, the service of the Lutheran Church, the orders of worship for the Methodist Church, the orders of worship from *The Book of Common Worship* of the Presbyterian Church, and others, all show a similarity of plan that follows rather closely the various steps in Isa., ch. 6.

As Charles Wolcott Merriam points out:

" In early Christian worship, in synagogue worship, and even in some of the more ancient temple ceremonies, the general plan of the service is much the same. It begins with a note of praise to create a realization of the presence of God. The next note is confession. . . . Its [worship's] next task is while retaining a sense of humility to rise to the altitude of assurance where the people can recite their beliefs and offer their prayers with a sense of pardon and the confidence of a new hope. . . . Next is the resolute expression of dedication. . . . [To this must be added] instruction and inspiration and here the sermon has its unrivaled opportunity." [32]

With this great weight of testimony, we may be sure that we have the pattern that, when used rightly, will stir men to sincere worship and to action. Our next concern is to be sure that the material, as well as the mold, is conducive to worship. The director must see that each item of his music is appropriate to and enhances the portion of worship in which it is used.

It behooves those who have the spiritual guidance of the people in their hands to give much time, study, and devotion to the planning of the worship services. Whether or not the worshipers see God in adoration, see themselves in humiliation, seek God's grace for purification, and give themselves through consecration rests to a great extent upon the selection and presentation of music in the church service.

15

THE ORGAN AND THE WORSHIP SERVICE

It is universally accepted that the pipe organ is the most suitable musical instrument to be used in public worship.[33] Because it is so sublime in tone and capable of such infinite variety in musical expression, it is the one instrument deemed proper to accompany the worshiper through all the reflections, meditations, and dedications of a service that includes adoration, humiliation, purification, and consecration. If the organ is going to be an aid to worship, it must be played by one who is both capable and consecrated. Much of the smooth flowing of the service is in the hands of the organist. He can greatly aid in the effectiveness of worship by judicious selections and artistic renditions. He must have a clear conception of what the service strives to accomplish. He must see that his music enhances the progression in worship.

The pastor, the choir director, and the organist form a trinity in leadership. Each must be devoted to the church, to its Head, and to the people it seeks to serve. Each must be a master in his own field. Each must understand his part in worship. Each must function in complete co-operation and sympathy with the others.

PRELUDE

The worship service begins with the first note of the
prelude. This is not a new idea to any church musician,
but it is still a new idea to many of the congregation and
the clergy. The use of the word " prelude " to identify
the organ music that is used at the beginning of a service
is unfortunate. The very word has given rise to the idea
that it is unimportant and not a part of the service itself;
the opposite is true. Dr. Waldo Seldon Pratt had the following to say regarding the prelude:

" The service prelude on the organ deserves fuller recognition than it sometimes receives. As the opening of
the service, it merits decorous attention from minister

and congregation, unbroken by the vulgarity of conversation or the disturbance of a stream of latecomers. Its
object is to suffuse a general atmosphere of reverence and
through the power of tone to knit together those present
into unity of feeling. Preludes, if the player be intent and
proper attention be accorded, have the power to intimate
much that is majestic, noble, gracious, and tender, couched
in terms of beauty that linger in the memory and touch the
spirit." [34]

I change the opening statement of this section: The
service begins when the first world-worn and seeking individual enters the silent sanctuary and there endeavors to
gain strength from the Infinite. For such a one the organ
music that we commonly call the prelude meets a real
need, whether you call it meditation, organ preparation,
the ministry of music, or what you will. It is for these worshipers that the organ prelude should begin softly, so
softly that they seem to feel the music before they hear it.
If the composition to be used does not so start, a short introduction can be improvised, starting with the softest
stops and building to the desired registration. If this is
done, there is no break or shock in the transition from a
quiet church to the service.

The ideal prelude is one that serves to clear the mind
of distraction, to direct the attention of the worshiper to
beauty, to lead him to a mood of reverence, and fittingly to
accompany his silent meditations.

OFFERTORY

The organ offertory is not intended merely as a cover
for the necessary confusion of the offering; it is another
occasion for ministry through music. Organists should

treat it thoughtfully. The music used should be within the line of the progression of the service. It must fit in with what has preceded and lead logically to the following numbers. For instance, if the choir sings near the organ offertory time, a composition from the same musical era or creative school may be used. The playing of a chorale prelude just before or after the choir's singing of the same melody in chorale form helps to bind the service together.

INTERLUDES

Another way of unifying the service musically and emotionally is in judicious use of organ interludes. It is unwise to improvise always; even the most skillful should do it sparingly. Hymn tunes suggesting appropriate words or seasons may be used. Phrases from anthems being sung in that service are effective. Have you considered the possibility of unifying the interludes throughout a service? Why not use, for instance, interludes entirely from *Elijah,* especially when the anthem is from that oratorio? Or interludes by Mendelssohn? One may use a portion of each of the following: " Lift Thine Eyes," " Cast Thy Burden," " Open the Heavens," and " O Rest in the Lord."

The same sort of thing can be done with other sacred works. Of course, it is important to work out all key relationships before the service. Sometimes this will involve the necessity of transposing a phrase into various keys.

HYMN PLAYING

When we think of the vital part religious song has played in the history of Christianity, we realize how important is hymn playing and singing in the church service. In announcing the tune, both mood and tempo should

be firmly established. Too many organists announce a
hymn in a slipshod and indifferent manner. Instead of
clean and accurate playing of four-part harmony, there
are apt to be omissions or additions. One makes for thin-
ness; the other, for muddiness. Hymn registration should
be carefully thought out and be in consonance with the
general character of the hymn. If it is a joyful hymn, use a
bright organ but not too loud, or it will discount the possibility of a climax later in the hymn. If it is a quiet, peaceful hymn, set this mood, but not so softly as to discourage
the congregation from singing. It is possible to build up a
bit at the end of the announcement of the hymn, as this
seems to invite the co-operation of singers. Legato playing
is imperative in most hymns. Beware of doubling by playing the bass part on the manuals and also on the pedals;
also beware of always playing the bass part an octave low.
In fact, there is a salutary effect in sometimes omitting all
pedal notes for a phrase or two. The low tones re-enter
with surprising vigor.

The amen following the hymn should be in keeping
with the general character of the hymn, and more particularly with the words of the concluding stanza. Avoid a
stereotyped, quiet amen. A triumphant amen is required
in such hymns as " Joyful, Joyful, We Adore Thee," concluding with:

> " Ever singing, march we onward,
>   Victors in the midst of strife,
> Joyful music leads us Sunward
>   In the triumph song of life. " [35]

Contrasting with the martial, stirring type of hymn is the
meditative hymn, as, for example, " Beneath the Cross of
Jesus," concluding with the words:

" My sinful self my only shame,
My glory all, the cross."

The first type of amen makes a triumphant, climactic ending for the hymn and leaves the congregation still singing
inwardly. The second type of amen seems to burn the
words in deeper, leaving the congregation in the attitude
of prayer and meditation.

Registration changes during the hymn must not be too
startling or too sentimental; for example, as in " Abide
with Me," playing " in life " fortissimo and " in death "
pianissimo. The congregation loses confidence in the organist when such liberties are taken. A judicious change
of registration in the progress of a hymn is advisable.[36]

POSTLUDE

The postlude is too often the weakest part of the service.
This is not necessarily because of a lack of preparation
by the organist, but rather because of the actions of the
congregation and clergy. Many organists, musicians, and
authorities in the art of worship are saying that either popular habits should be reformed or postludes given up entirely.

The use of fantasies on familiar hymn tunes sometimes
leads to more interest on the part of the congregation, as
they hear strains they recognize.

REPERTOIRE

In selecting repertoire, the organist will find a few general rules serving as guides:

He must refrain from using cheap music and music un-
suited to the organ. Popular songs or trivial piano pieces

full of runs or arpeggios are not suited either to the organ
or to the church.

Music with definite secular association should be
avoided. A church bulletin recently came to the writer's
notice that carried " My Heart at Thy Sweet Voice " as the
organ offertory number. This aria from *Samson and De-
lilah* not only takes the congregation out of the church and
into the opera house, but it brings before them one of the
most sensual characters in history in, according to the
opera, her most passionate love song. This is hardly worship music. In fact, the use of any opera selection is in
doubtful taste, even though it may be beautiful, restful,
or religious. To some it will suggest the opera, not worship.
Thus there is much fine music that is not recommended
because of the associations that are suggested.

Avoid hackneyed music. A congregation is always fond
of familiar music, but some is so common that it ought
not to be used. Each organist should make his own list of
" too common " numbers. In it he would surely put Handel's " Largo," " Traumerei," by Schumann, and " Melody
in F," by Rubenstein. If the people insist on these, have a
special program for them and play all their favorite re-
quests, but do not call it a worship service.

Avoid showy music. The *Manual of Presbyterian Law*
says: " The introduction of choirs or musical instruments
can be justified only as they serve this end (of inspiring
and expressing devotion) and aid or accompany sacred
song; and no display of artistic skill, no delicacy of vocal
training, no measure of musical ability, compensates for
the violation, or even neglect, of the proprieties of divine
worship." Most church bodies have some such official statement. The desire to display one's abilities is a laudable am-
bition, but this desire should be fulfilled outside the

church service. The display of one's abilities distracts from worship. It should be remembered that the display of one's lack of ability also distracts from worship. The individual must be in the background.

What, then, should be used? Music written for the church service by an organist who has given a lifetime to church organ playing will probably be found worthy of use. But put the test to it: Does it lead to " devotion, adoration, reverence, awe, mystery, and aspiration "? If the music meets these tests and is played by an organist whose attitude toward his profession is dignified and devotional, the music can hardly fail in its purpose.

16

THE CHOIR AND THE
WORSHIP SERVICE

VESTMENTS

The observant director is conscious of a revival of interest in beauty and symbolism in Protestant worship. Many denominations have recommended that the churches take steps to make their services more effective by appealing to the aesthetic sense of man as well as his spiritual instincts. Religious art, ecclesiastical symbols, and colors are gradually being returned to the institution that all but abandoned their use when it was transplanted from the Old World to the New. It is earnestly hoped that Protestantism may learn how to use beauty, in all its forms, as an aid to worship, but not make beauty the end in itself.

In making provision for the choirs, the director must take into consideration an appropriate dress or vestment for them. He should make a decision as to what is proper only after reflection on the history of vestments, the significance of their various parts, and the symbolic use of color. The decision, too, should take into account the nature of the church he is serving. Is it a liturgical church or a free church, a high church or a low church, or has it an intermediary degree of altitude?

Why Use Vestments?

The most apparent reason why we recommend vestments for a choir is for the sake of uniformity of appearance. Variety in clothes in the choir loft calls attention to the individuals and distracts from the oneness that should be evidenced as the message of Christianity is sung. A heterogeneous group is made to feel its unity by a uniform

dress. This is as it should be for a company leading in corporate worship.

It has been commonly felt over the centuries that the reverence and dignity appropriate to the worship of God finds suitable expression in the wearing of a distinctive dress by those who lead in worship. In the twenty-eighth chapter of Exodus, the Mosaic law gave strict directions as to the vestments to be worn by the Jewish priests. The early Christian church, because of the very nature of its uncertain and perilous existence, did not have its leaders wear a distinguishing garb. They wore the dress common to all the men of their time, the classical Roman costume. This style gradually changed, and after the fourth century

the common people adopted a more military dress. The
priests, however, retained the classical toga. From this
raiment the elaborate vestments of the Eastern and Western church gradually were developed. Protestantism in
general never has felt the necessity of having its ministers
wear a distinguishing dress at all times. It has, however,
sensed that its worship leaders, both ministerial and musical, should wear symbolic apparel during their ministrations.

The most commonly used vestment for choristers in the
liturgical churches is the cassock with surplice or cotta. In
some churches a stole or girdle is worn. The loosely hang-
ing gown is primarily an academic garb, it has little religious significance, and historically should be used only
on scholastic occasions. It must be added, however, that
this gown has become the accepted vestment for many
churches, particularly those of the nonliturgical order.
It may well be that this will become the universally accepted dress for the nonritualistic ministerial and choral
leaders.

Symbolism of Vestments and Colors

The cassock and cotta or the flowing robe suggest the
acceptance of priestly responsibilities. The girdle suggests
action or service. The stole typifies the yoke of Christ
which the wearer has assumed in ministering to the people.

In selecting colors for choir vestments, the director
should keep in mind the ecclesiastical symbolism of colors.
From the earliest recorded times, religion has used color
in its worship as a legitimate appeal to the sense of beauty
through the eye. The Protestant Church is all too slow in
recovering from the Puritanic drabness imposed upon it
by our well-meaning but aesthetically insensible fore-

fathers. But there is a reaction, and color is being returned to the church.

The most common liturgical colors are white, red, green, violet, and black.

White is used to symbolize Deity. It also suggests purity of heart and Christians' joy.

Red, the color of blood, typifies life, love, enthusiasm, creative power, and the masculine principle. Blue is sometimes used for the feminine principle. Red also suggests the fire of the Holy Spirit and the blood of the martyrs.

Green is emblematic of nature, being its commonest color. Green signifies fertility, hope, life, and immortality.

Violet is the penitential color and is used in liturgical churches, chiefly during Advent and Lent.

Black should be used ecclesiastically only at funerals and on Good Friday, unless it is covered by the white of Deity, as in the use of a black cassock and white surplice. Black symbolizes the evil principle; it also stands for night, chaos, death. In not such a depressing symbolism, it represents sleep and rest.

No matter what type of vestment is selected for the choir, no matter what color is used, it is very important that the vestments themselves, whether rich and costly or plain and simple, should not lack the beauty, dignity, and good taste that are becoming to garments set apart for use in the worship of the church of God. A vestment is not just a uniform to be worn by the choristers. It is an evidence that the wearer has been deemed worthy to be a leader and is so appointed by his church. It links the choristers to those of all the ages who have led in the worship of God. It is part of the ceremony of the church. But a ceremony is not mere show. It is symbolic language by which the heart of man expresses his sense of the mystery, the holiness, and

the splendor of the triune God; his aspirations for high
things; his reverence; his hope of glory.

THE ANTHEM

When one thinks of the music peculiar to the choir, he
first thinks of the anthem.[37] The word " anthem " is derived from the word " antiphon." This word suggests the
more common word " antiphonal." The first antiphons or
anthems were a type of responsive singing: choir answering choir, or choir answering priests. The word " anthem "
in modern use has almost completely lost this responsive-
singing meaning. An anthem is a musical composition set
to words of sacred character intended for use in divine
services by a choir. In earlier times, only words from Scripture or the liturgies were considered appropriate; in recent
days, any words of a reverent nature may be the basis of
an anthem. The music of the anthem has changed con-
siderably from its early forms. At its beginning it varied
but slightly from a psalm or hymn tune. It has progressed
through many stages of musical development until now
it may be cast in an elaborate musical mold.

That the choir should render offerings to God in the
form of anthems is highly desirable, but they must be
worthy and sincere acts of worship on its part. An anthem
to be suitable for this use must possess certain qualities.
These have been discussed in Chapter 12. In addition it
must be used in the portion of the service in which it fits
emotionally. If an anthem of praise is sung in the humiliation section of the service, say after the call to confession,
the anthem will fail to invoke praise. If an anthem of consecration is used in the adoration portion, it will not move
the hearers to greater dedication; they are not prepared

for it. The anthem should not always be sung in the same place in the service unless it always has the same emotional feeling. If the anthem is regularly sung before the prayer, it should consistently be a prayer anthem. The anthem's only reason for use is to intensify the mood of the portion of worship in which it is used. It will do this only if it is closely knit, both in thought and in feeling, to the surrounding parts of the service. Dr. Pratt expresses this admirably when he writes:

" The text of every anthem needs to be carefully weighed as to its general sense and predominant tone. If it be an utterance of ecstatic jubilance or triumph or even of extreme confession or entreaty, particularly if these qualities are heightened by the musical treatment (as they ought to be), it is clear that such an anthem should not be inserted in any service except in a place where it will seem to grow naturally out of its immediate surroundings and where by some means the minds of the congregation have been prepared to adopt it as substantially their own. The reckless insertion of such musical praise or prayer works only liturgical imbecility." [38]

CHANTS AND LITURGICAL MUSIC

In churches of the liturgical group, one of the chief functions of the choir is to lead in the singing of the psalms and canticles. Theoretically, this type of music has an extensive congregational participation. Practically, it is left to the choir to perform. The music used with the psalms and canticles is a combination of measured and unmeasured music; that is to say, one portion is sung in a definite rhythmical order, the other portion is sung without any fixed succession or relation of musical accents. This type of music is called a chant.

The history of the chant takes one back to Saint Ambrose, A.D. 340?–397. Doubtless the psalms were intoned, a
form of chanting, at a much earlier date. Each age and
church that appropriated the chant made some alterations
in its form and use.

The two principal schools of chanting are the Gregorian
and the Anglican. The Gregorian chant used in the Roman
Catholic Church was developed by Saint Gregory (540?–
604). The Anglican chant was evolved in the Church of
England in the Middle Ages. When the psalms and canticles are well chanted, an ethereal quality is added to the
worship service that has always moved man toward his
Creator.

Though chanting is chiefly associated with the liturgies
of the Roman Catholic, Anglican, and Protestant Episcopal Churches, other churches not infrequently call upon
their choirs to chant.[39] The hymnbooks of most denominations contain some psalms and canticles pointed for chanting.

CHORAL RESPONSES

Choral calls to worship, introits, calls to prayer, prayer
responses, and offertory sentences provide the choir with
opportunities for effective worship and musical expressions. The director should have many choral sentences
ready to use with the choirs in the various worship services. He may select responses from the multiplicity of material issued by music publishers; he will find a section of
responses in most church hymnals; he will also find that
there are many phrases from anthems and hymns that are
suitable for this use.

Hymn phrases seem to be particularly helpful to the congregation as prayer responses. The strain of a familiar hymn ties the worshiper to the prayer and also invokes from him a memory response. Let the director consider as prayer responses such phrases as: " Spirit of holiness, on us descend," from " Come, Thou Almighty King "; " Come, cast your burdens on the Lord, and trust His constant care," from " How Gentle God's Commands "; " Let me hide myself in Thee," from " Rock of Ages "; " All other ground is sinking sand," from " My Hope Is Built on Nothing Less "; and many other appropriate ones. These points of musical ministration, i.e., the responses and sentences, are often treated too casually by both director and choir. They are worthy of more consideration than they customarily receive.[40]

If the choir does not sing a recessional, it might be well to consider singing a choral postlude instead of or in addition to the organ postlude. What could be more appropriate than that as the people leave the sanctuary they should carry with them the strains of a familiar hymn or anthem? One or two stanzas of " Lead On, O King Eternal," " Rise Up, O Men of God! " " Let All the World in Every Corner Sing," " O for a Thousand Tongues to Sing," or any one of a number of hymns can tellingly crystallize the mood of a service. Many times the climax pages of an anthem of praise sung earlier in the service are appropriate for use as a choral postlude.

PROCESSIONAL

Although the congregation may sing on all or part of the processional and recessional hymns, the choir carries the burden of their effective rendition.

Why should we have a processional? It furnishes a dramatic and convincing way of bringing the choir and the minister into the sanctuary. Instead of sauntering in and waiting for the service to begin, they bring the service with them as they sing the processional hymn. The processional symbolizes the calls to worship: " Let us go into the house of the Lord," and " O come, let us sing unto the Lord." It quickly makes a heterogeneous group of people into a congregation of worshipers as they unite in spiritual song. The processional can tellingly introduce the first element necessary in a worship service, the adoration of God. It adds color and pageantry that the church will be wise to cultivate.

In the light of these reasons for the processional, great care must be taken to perfect every detail of it. The processional must be orderly and precise; with this there can be no compromise. That the choir will be vested is a foregone conclusion. It will help in the appearance of the choir if the singers all hold the hymnbooks in the same manner. The books may be held in any way that is convenient, as long as the impression is not artificial.

The choir members should keep step in their processionals. They must walk rhythmically, two steps to a measure in common time. One extra measure of silence, while the organ holds the last chord, is recommended at the end of each stanza. Step with the left foot as the first beat in each measure is sung. The singers must walk erect with good posture and without swaying. They must use an unpretentious walking step, no " waltz steps," " glide steps," " wedding march " or " goose steps." Through all processing, the emphasis is upon an orderliness and precision that is in keeping with the dignity and mission of the church.

The Catholic and High Episcopal Churches, with their

slow-walking processionals, are perpetuating the custom of the churches of an earlier age. In that day the procession to the church was led by the priest, who intoned the litany, and the people sang the responses as they followed. The music of the time was unrhythmic, and so a marching processional was impossible. That type of processional is hardly in keeping with the spirit of the modern Protestant Church.

If used sparingly, a silent processional or a processional with quiet organ music but without singing is very effective. It is especially impressive during Lent, at Communion services, Holy Week services, and choir dedication services.

An effective method of adding interest and fervor to the processional hymns (or to other hymns at special times) is by the occasional use of descants.[41] The descant is an independent melody above the main melody of a hymn. It is usually sung by the sopranos of the choir as all others, both of the choir and congregation, sing the melody of the hymn in unison. The descant is an old church form that has been revived effectively in this century. A descant should be sung on not more than two stanzas of a hymn, of which one must be the last stanza.

In the processional we process from the world into the church for worship; in the recessional we process into the world again for service. All that was said regarding the processional is equally applicable to the recessional. They must both be executed with stateliness and decorum in a manner befitting the onward-marching church of God.

CONGREGATIONAL MUSIC IN THE
WORSHIP SERVICE

Protestantism rose to power on the inspiring strains of the congregational hymn. Luther, Calvin, Hus, and other Reformers might not have gained an extensive following through their theological insurrections alone. These men sensed the stimulating power of group singing. They made a large place for congregational expression in " psalms and hymns and spiritual songs."

The hymn was written for the people; in it they express their prayer and praise, their adoration and consecration. In it they find strength and courage for the trials of life. In the hymn they may directly address God, or they may meditate upon the Christian way of living. The hymn is the people's expression of Christianity. Good hymn singing is their obligation and privilege toward the development of effective public worship. The people, the minister, and the musical director must work together to make hymn singing a vital part of worship and the power it should be in the life of the church.

In churches where there is good congregational singing, it is never an accident. Someone has sown the seed which is now blooming in expressive, wholehearted song.

TOWARD BETTER HYMN SINGING

If the hymn singing in your church is not all you think it should be, check up on the following points:

Are the children and young people in the church school and youth societies being taught the great hymns, those which have stood the test of generations of usage and which they will sing in a lifetime of church attendance? This is where your congregations and choirs of the future are being molded. If your people do not sing well now, it may be because they were not taught great Christian songs in their youth. You may be reaping another's poor sowing. The song leaders in the various church school departments may appreciate a few suggestions as to suitable hymns and methods of teaching and presenting them. The youth choirs should regularly be taught several hymns a season. Memory hymn contests may be conducted.

Does the organist know how to play hymns? It is astonishing, but there are many organists who can play the difficult music of the Franck, Guilmant, and Sowerby type but who have never learned to play hymns. It is likely that they realize neither the difficulties nor the importance of good hymn playing. The organist sets the tempo. It should be neither too slow nor too fast; the music will drag, or the congregation will not be able to keep up. Too much organ drowns out the singers; too little will make the congregation self-conscious as they hear their own voices alone. A sudden change from forte to pianissimo gives a congregation the feeling of having been suspended in mid-air, and they will stop singing. When this happens a few times, it will make the singers suspicious, and they will refuse to sing at all. Too much use of solo stops or the bringing out of inner voices too prominently tends to form an uncertain background for the congregationally sung hymn. The accompanist should breathe with the singers; especially is this necessary between stanzas.

Wrath — but holy wrath, if you please — is incited by those organists who precede each stanza with the first melody note one beat ahead, and the ones who play a little interlude before the last stanza, and those who take it upon themselves to reharmonize the hymn, often changing it with each stanza!

Is the choir giving enough time to the preparation of the hymns so that it can lead the singing of them correctly? Familiar hymns are sung reasonably well, but when the pastor, becoming bold, schedules a new hymn, what happens? Most choirs are not good enough readers to sing a new hymn correctly on first sight and at the same time lead the congregation. The congregation, waiting for the choir's lead, which has failed, hesitates to sing, and the new hymn fares badly. The pastor decides that he had better select the " old hymns," not remembering that the " old hymns " were once " new hymns." On the other hand, if the organist introduces the new hymn well, and the choir, having studied it in rehearsal, leads confidently, the bold venture may not go too poorly.

Are the people instructed, whenever the opportunity presents itself, to sing the hymns in unison? From the time of the early church, a single melodic line has been considered the best medium for the vocal utterance of the congregation. This is not necessarily because of the inability of the congregation to sing in parts, but rather because the unison singing of hymns is best suited for the purposes of worship. A firm melody is much more effective for all concerned than wavering part singing. The confirmed part singer may grumble a dissenting vote, saying that anyone can sing the melody, or the bass may say that the melody is too high. Let the dissenter sing his part, urge all others to sing the melody, and let the organ supply the harmonic fullness.

If authorities for unison singing are desired, the following should suffice:

John Wesley printed the tunes of the hymns only, without harmony, for the people's use. He exhorted them to "learn these tunes."

When John Calvin entrusted to Louis Bourgeois the composing of new tunes for the *Genevan Psalter,* he made but two stipulations: the tunes must be sung in unison, and there must be only one note to each syllable.

Dr. Sydney Nicholson says, "Many will admit, I think rightly, that congregational singing can, to be artistic, only be in unison: no artistic result can be obtained by promiscuous attempts at harmony by an ordinary congregation where the voices at best must be ill-balanced, and at worst, are hopelessly incorrect." [42]

Canon Winfred Douglas writes of the hymnbook *Songs of Praise,* "Indeed, the editors direct that the 'congregation must always sing the melody, and the melody only,' wise and sound advice." [43]

Dr. Robert G. McCutchan writes: "Why do we persist in encouraging our congregations (if we encourage them at all) to sing in parts? When are we going to encourage the singing of the melody in unison by our congregations? It ought to solve some of our difficulties." [44]

If the congregation is going to be expected to sing the melody only, and enjoy doing so, we must see to it that the key of the hymn does not give any high notes. A mixed congregation should never be expected to sing above E (fourth space, treble staff). If D is the upper limit, the hymn is more apt to be well sung. A study of recent hymn-

books reveals a decided trend toward lowering the keys of
hymns that contained high notes.

Are the hymns selected good hymns, from both word
and music standpoints? That the hymn should be carefully
and prayerfully selected seems self-evident, but often the
choosing of the hymn is left to a haphazard opening of the
book. If the church is using the authorized hymnal of its
denomination, one can be reasonably certain that any
hymn therein is worthy of use. If any other book is used,
one cannot trust it so completely. When judging the worth
of a hymn, use the measure that Dr. Louis F. Benson, the
hymnologist, laid down.[45] He said that a hymn should have
lyric qualities, literary excellence, liturgical propriety,
reverence, and spiritual reality.

Are the people taught hymnology? Do they know what
is in the hymnal? There are many occasions when the musical director or pastor can say a few words about a hymn
that will add immensely to the joy and understanding in
singing it. For instance, it is surprising that a large majority of worshiping Christians, even though they have
sung " Come, Thou Almighty King " all their lives, have
never noticed that each of the first three stanzas is addressed to one of the Trinity, and that the fourth stanza
is addressed to the Trinity as a whole. Few realize that
when we sing " Art Thou Weary, Art Thou Languid? "
we are bridging a gulf of eleven hundred years and using a
paraphrased hymn originally written by a monk of the
Eastern Church in the monastery of Mar Saba in the wil-
derness of Judea.

WHAT DOES THE HYMNAL OFFER?

What is really to be found between the covers of this
book that we handle so thoughtlessly? Poetry is there,

music is there, religion is there, history is there, romance is there, the heartbeats of many lives are to be found there.

The one who neglects the hymnbook neglects a broad education that is easily available and very thrilling to study. In the hymnbook you meet most of the great poets from David through Addison, Milton, Tennyson, Bryant, Cowper, Bunyan, Whittier, Longfellow, Lowell, Holmes, to Oxenham and the contemporary poets.

In the hymnbook you will find many of the great composers, from Palestrina through Bach, Handel, Haydn, Mendelssohn, Beethoven, Mozart, Gounod, Sullivan, to Gustav Holst, Horatio Parker, and Vaughan Williams.

If you are interested in musical form, you will find the plain song or chant of the early church; you will find chorales, part songs, folk tunes; you will find arrangements from symphonies, symphonic poems, operas, piano pieces, and oratorios.

You will find some of the organizers of great church groups there — witness Luther and the Wesleys. The religious philosophies and to some extent the doctrines of all orthodox groups will be found there.

You will find the intensely devotional songs that were sung by the early Christians in the catacombs, the ethereal chants of Saint Ambrose from the early Roman service, sturdy chorales of the Reformation, stately hymns of the English cathedral, lyrics of the social-conscious twentieth century, and gospel songs of the nineteenth century.

You will find greater human interest stories than you can find in fiction. You will find the lives of hundreds of men and women spread before you.

The greatest single book collection of poetry, music, religion, history, philosophy, and romance ever compiled is in the hands of the members of the congregation as they hold their hymnbooks to sing. Teach them something of hymnology, and they will sing with more zest and understanding.[46]

Are the hymns selected with the emotional line of the service in mind? A hymn may be a fine one, but if it is used in a part of the service that does not accord with its emotional tone, it will never be well sung. Like the anthem, it must have an agreement with the portions of the service to which it is adjacent. Do not schedule " Fairest Lord Jesus " to be sung just after a call to confession, or " O Worship the King " just before the pastoral prayer, and expect them to be sung well.

About the middle of the last century a new type of religious song began to be developed. It may be called the popular religious song, in contrast to the classical, similar to the popular secular song in contradistinction to the classical secular. The words had scant literary quality, and often the religious truths were clothed in the most flippant phrases. The tunes composed for these lyrics had little musical value. Written with a popular rhythmic swing and with catchy, tawdry melodies, they displayed little of dignity, of reverence, or of a devotional mood. They were called " gospel songs." This title was unfortunate, for it in no way suggested their true character or style, but we shall have to use it because of its common acceptance. Of course many who wrote gospel songs wrote seriously and gave their best efforts to the form. Doubtless these songs filled an important need in the popular evangelistic meeting and camp-meeting day. It is an accepted fact that many people would testify to the spiritual help received from the gospel song, so one has no right to condemn *in toto* all songs of this type.

The very fact that this type of song is on the decline in

usage in our churches shows that as a class it has not the permanent value that we find in the more dignified hymns. We do, however, find some of these songs in most hymn-books and probably shall continue to find them, for some have been quite generally accepted and mean much to some people. The best of them, use sparingly; they are poor substitutes for good hymns. The poorest of them, shun; they are cheap, tawdry, and unworthy to be used in the worship of God.

The congregation's musical participation in the worship service usually includes, aside from the regular type of hymns, the Gloria Patri and/or Ken's Doxology.

THE GLORIA PATRI

The Gloria Patri is one of the very oldest expressions of Christian praise. Some writers think that the first part — " Glory be to the Father, and to the Son, and to the Holy Ghost " — may have had its origin at the time of the apostles themselves. It is certain that it was used before A.D. 300.[47] The second half — " As it was in the beginning, is now, and ever shall be, world without end " — was added sometime later, probably in the fourth century. By the end of the fourth century the Gloria Patri was an established part of the Christian worship.

The Gloria's traditional place of use is at the end of the reading or chanting of a psalm. The early church, follow-ing the example of Jewish practice in the Temple, used the psalter in its worship. Soon the church added to each psalm the enduring stanza of the Gloria Patri, thus mak-ing a Jewish song of praise equally applicable to the Fa-ther, Son, or Holy Ghost.

Christians, the world around, unite each Sabbath in

this ancient utterance of praise. In its brief phrases are expressed the great doctrines upon which the church was founded and has grown. In it Christians reaffirm " their belief in the triune God of the past, the present, and ageless eternity." [48]

THE DOXOLOGY

Bishop Thomas Ken, in 1695, wrote three hymns [49] for the boys of Winchester College (England) had ended each with the same stanza:

> " Praise God, from whom all blessings flow;
> Praise Him, all creatures here below;
> Praise Him above, ye heavenly host:
> Praise Father, Son, and Holy Ghost."

At that time Bishop Ken could hardly have envisioned that he was giving to the Christian world the third in a trinity of doxologies. As far as Protestantism was concerned it was the one destined to be the most universally used. The first- or second-century hymn of Greek origin, Gloria in Excelsis Deo, is known to hymnologists as " the greater doxology"; the Gloria Patri is referred to as " the lesser doxology "; Ken's doxology completes the trio.

H. Augustine Smith says of Ken's stanza of divine approbation: " Ken's Doxology is a masterpiece at once of amplification and compression: of amplification on the thought, ' Praise God,' repeated in every line; of compression, by including, in the short space of four lines, God as the object of praise for all his blessings, by every creature, above, below, and in each of his manifestations as Father, Son, and Holy Ghost." [50]

This Doxology, with its customarily used music of the

tune " Old Hundredth," is most effective as the climax of the ritual of the worship service. Though it is used in the early part of services in some churches, authorities on worship feel that it is most appropriate when used in connection with the presentation of the offering. In the offering the congregation gives outward evidence of its consecration and loyalty and its willingness to serve its Master. In the offering one symbolically presents himself as he presents his money. It is most befitting that at such a time he should stand and heartily sing this paean to God, the Father, Son, and Holy Spirit.

18

GENERAL MUSICAL SERVICES
OF WORSHIP

A musical service that interprets a theme has more value than an unrelated collection of anthems, no matter how fine the music or how well performed. A minister would not take an unconnected series of thoughts and illustrations and, putting them together, consider that he had a sermon. No more should the musician assemble miscellaneous music and consider that he has a musical service of worship. A concert of sacred music? Possibly. A service? No.

In the services here outlined, music was used to amplify a subject. In most of the services there were also some of the regular parts of worship: Scripture, prayers, hymns, and a sermon. However, only the items that apply directly to the subject are listed.

Of course each service idea can be interpreted in many ways and with a wide variety of musical selections. All the themes given here, and the music indicated, have been used by the writer.

To designate which age choirs used the anthems, the words " Adult," " Children," or " Combined " will be found. Titles, composers, and publishers of all anthems are listed.

A MUSICAL INTERPRETATION OF THE APOSTLES' CREED
(All anthems were sung by the adult choir)

" I believe in God the Father Almighty, Maker of heaven and earth; "

  " Holy Lord God "   Cain (Flammer)

" And in Jesus Christ his only Son our Lord; "

  " Beautiful Savior "   Christiansen (Augsburg)

" Who was conceived by the Holy Ghost, born of the Virgin Mary,"

  " Sleep of the Child Jesus "   Gevaert (G. Schirmer)

" Suffered under Pontius Pilate, was crucified, dead, and buried; "

  " Were You There When They Crucified My Lord? "

           Burleigh (Ricordi)

" He descended into hell; the third day he rose again from the dead; "

  " A Russian Easter Alleluia "   Gaul (G. Schirmer)

" He ascended into heaven, and sitteth on the right hand of God the Father Almighty; from thence he shall come to judge the quick and the dead."

  " Unfold Ye Portals " (Redemption)

          Gounod (G. Schirmer)

" I believe in the Holy Ghost; "

  " Send Forth Thy Spirit "   Schuetky (Birchard)

" The holy catholic church; "

  " Built on a Rock "   Christiansen (Augsburg)

" The communion of saints; "

  Hymn — " Blest Be the Tie That Binds "   Fawcett

" The forgiveness of sins; "

  " O Thou from Whom All Blessings Come "

        Tschaikowsky (E. C. Schirmer)

" The resurrection of the body; "
    Solo " I Know that My Redeemer Liveth " (Messiah)
                              Handel (G. Schirmer)

" And the life everlasting. Amen."
   " God So Loved the World "   Stainer (G. Schirmer)

A Musical Interpretation of the Affirmation of Faith

" We believe in the one God, Maker and Ruler of all things,
Father of all men, the source of all goodness and beauty, all
truth and love."
    Hymn — " Now Thank We All Our God "   Rinkart

" We believe in Jesus Christ, God manifest in the flesh, our
Teacher, Example, and Redeemer, the Saviour of the world."
    Children: " O Saviour Sweet "   Bach (Gray)

" We believe in the Holy Spirit, God present with us for guidance, for comfort, and for strength."
    Adult: " Come Thou Holy Spirit "   Tschesnokoff (Kjos)

" We believe in the forgiveness of sins, in the life of love and
prayer, and in grace equal to every need."
    Adult: " O Thou from Whom All Blessings Come "
                  Tschaikowsky (E. C. Schirmer)

" We believe in the Word of God contained in the Old and
New Testaments as the sufficient rule both of faith and of
practice."
    Children: Hymn — " Thy Word Is like a Garden, Lord "
                            Hodder

" We believe in the Church as the fellowship for worship and
for service of all who are united to the Living Lord."
    Adult: " Built on a Rock "   Christiansen (Augsburg)

" We believe in the kingdom of God as the divine rule in human society; and in the brotherhood of man under the Father-
hood of God."
    Adult: " Worship "   Shaw (Novello)

" We believe in the final triumph of righteousness, and in the life everlasting. Amen."

Combined: " The Day of Resurrection "

Mueller (C. Fischer)

EACH NEW SEASON SPEAKS TO US OF GOD

Hymn — " This Is My Father's World "   Babcock

Prologue

Children: " A Child's Thanksgiving "   Baynon (Oxford)

Summer — Nature

Children: " I So Often Wonder "   Jones (C. Fischer)
Adult: " As Torrents in Summer "   Elgar (Novello)

Autumn — Thanksgiving

Adult: " Bless the Lord, O My Soul "

Ippolitof-Ivanof (Boston)

Winter — Christmas

Combined: " As It Fell Upon a Night "   Davies (Galaxy)

Spring — Palm Sunday and Easter

Adult: " Hosanna! Blessed Is He "   Marryott (Ditson)
Combined: " One Early Easter Morning "   Marryott (Ditson)

HEREIN IS GOD REVEALED TO MAN

Through Worship

Children: " O Come Let Us Worship "   Mueller (Morris)

Through History

Adult: " Hymn of the Pilgrims "   MacDowell (Schmidt)
Combined: " Thanks Be to Thee "   Handel (J. Fischer)

Through the Lives of Men

Children: " Now Praise We Great and Famous Men "
Mueller (Flammer)

Through Nature

Adult: " The Heavens Are Telling "
Beethoven (E. C. Schirmer)
Children: " We Tread Upon Thy Carpets "
Whittlesey (Flammer)

Through the Bible

Children: Hymn — " Book of Books, Our People's Strength "
Dearmer

Through Jesus Christ

Combined: " Beautiful Savior "   Christiansen (Augsburg)

PRAISE TO THE ETERNAL GOD

Adult (with Reader) : " Let Us Praise God "
Olds (Hall & McCreary)

For Himself

Adult: " God Himself Is with Us "   Bitgood (Gray)

For the Good Shepherd

Children: " Brother James' Air "   Jacob (Oxford)

For the Daily Blessings of Life

Children: " A Child's Prayer "   Taylor (Oxford)
Children: " God, Who Touchest Earth with Beauty "
Mueller (Morris)
Combined: " O Come Let Us Sing Unto the Lord "
Mueller (C. Fischer)
Hymn — " Praise Ye the Lord, the Almighty, the King of Crea-
tion! "
Neander

A Service of Psalms

Organ: Choral Prelude — " Ach Gott, vom Himmel sich dar-
ein "   (Psalm 22)   Hanff (Peters)
Psalm 18   Marcello (Gray)
Intermezzo (Psalm 37:38)   Whitlock (Oxford)
Hymn — " Jesus Shall Reign Where'er the Sun "   Watts
(In this hymn Isaac Watts took the 72d Psalm and trans-
formed it into a celebration of the conquest of Christ among
the heathen. The psalm has been " imitated in the spirit of
Christianity.")

Psalm 100

Combined: " Make a Joyful Noise Unto the Lord "
Mueller (Flammer)

Psalm 24

Responsive Reading: The youth choirs recite the verses usually read by the minister.

Psalm 103

Adult: " Bless Thou the Lord, O My Soul "   Ivanof (Boston)

Psalm 23

Children: " Brother James' Air "   Jacob (Oxford)
(The words are the 1650 Scottish Psalter version of the
psalm.)

Psalm 27

Children: " The Lord Is My Light and My Salvation "
Protheroe (FitzSimons)

Psalm 150

Combined: " Psalm One Hundred and Fifty "
Franck (Ditson)
Hymn — " Praise Ye the Lord, the Almighty, the King of Crea-
tion! "   Neander

(This hymn is based on Psalms 103 and 150.)
Hymn — " O God, Our Help in Ages Past "   Watts
(This hymn is based on Psalm 90.)

Jesus Shall Reign

Hymn — " Jesus Shall Reign Where'er the Sun "   Watts

In Our Nation

Adult: " Hymn of the Pilgrims "   MacDowell (Schmidt)

In Our Church

Adult: " Let Us Break Bread Together "
                                        Marshall (C. Fischer)

In Our Homes

Children: " Prayer of the Norwegian Child "
                                        Kountz (G. Schirmer)

In Our Hearts

Adult: " O Come to My Heart, Lord Jesus "
                                        Ambrose (Ditson)

Where'er the Sun

Combined: " All Hail the Power of Jesus' Name "
                                Shrubsole-Ward (Flammer)
Hymn — " Fairest Lord Jesus "

Worship Through Music Commemorating Our Protestant Heritage

Organ and Brass Quartet: " Sleepers, Wake " (Sunrise on
Easter Morning)   Bach-Olds (C. Fischer)
Hymn — " The Church's One Foundation "   Stone
Combined: " The Sanctus "   Luther-Dickinson (Gray)
Adult: " We All Believe in One True God "
                                        Mueller (C. Fischer)

Children: " Ah Dearest Jesus "   Luther (Various)
Responsive Reading: Psalm 46
   (This psalm was the inspiration for Luther's great hymn,
   " A Mighty Fortress Is Our God.")
Combined (with Brass Quartet) : " How Brightly Shines the
Morning Star "   Nicolai-Olds (C. Fischer)
Scripture Lesson
   (Compiled from texts used by Luther in his Sermon on
   Galatians.)
Combined: " A Mighty Fortress Is Our God "
                Luther-Olds (Hall & McCreary)
Hymn — " Now Thank We All Our God "   Rinkart

GOD'S SEVEN FREEDOMS

As Promised in the Twenty-third Psalm

(This outline was suggested by the Freedoms Foundation of
the National Association of Evangelicals.)

Freedom from Want

" The Lord is my shepherd; I shall not want."
Children: " God Watches Over All the World "
                Kettring (Gray)

Freedom from Hunger

" He maketh me to lie down in green pastures: "
Combined: " List to the Lark "   Dickinson (Gray)

Freedom from Thirst

" He leadeth me beside the still waters."
Scripture Reading from John, ch. 4 — The Water of Life

Freedom from Sin

" He restoreth my soul:
  He leadeth me in the paths of righteousness for his name's
  sake."
Combined: " Lead Me, Lord "   Wesley (E. C. Schirmer)

Freedom from Fear

" Yea, though I walk through the valley of the shadow of death,
I will fear no evil: for thou art with me;
Thy rod and thy staff they comfort me."
Adult: " The Silent Sea "　　　　　　Neidlinger (G. Schirmer)

Freedom from Danger

" Thou preparest a table before me in the presence of mine
enemies: "
Adult: " For All Who Watch "　　　　　　Dickinson (Gray)

Freedom to Live Abundantly

" Thou anointest my head with oil; my cup runneth over.
Surely goodness and mercy shall follow me all the days of
my life:
And I will dwell in the house of the Lord for ever."
Combined: " Thanks Be to Thee "　　　　Handel (J. Fischer)

IN HIS STEPS

" Follow with reverent steps the great example
Of Him whose holy work was doing good." — Whittier.

In Devotion to God

" But I do as the Father has commanded me, so that the world
may know that I love the Father." — John 14:31.
Adult: " My Eternal King "　　　　　　Marshall (C. Fischer)

In Inner Peace and Trust

" Peace I leave with you; my peace I give to you; . . . Let
not your hearts be troubled, neither let them be afraid."
　　　　　　　　　　　　　　　　　— John 14:27.
Children: " Prayer "　　　　Humperdinck (G. Schirmer)
Adult: " It Is a Precious Thing "　　　Peter-Dickinson (Gray)

In Service to Man

" I am among you as one who serves." — Luke 22:27.

Children: " A Child's Prayer "   Taylor (Oxford)
Adult: " I Bind My Heart "   Marshall (C. Fischer)
Adult: " Rise Up, O Men of God "   Reed (J. Fischer)

In Prayer

" Pray then like this." — Matt. 6:9.

Combined: " The Lord's Prayer "   Malotte (G. Schirmer)

THE EARTHLY LIFE OF OUR LORD

Birth

Combined: " Christ Came to Bethlehem "   Williams (Gray)

Ministry

Adult: " The Great Commandments "   Mueller (C. Fischer)

Triumph

Combined: " Prepare the Way to Zion "   Luvaas (Ditson)

Death

Children: " The Knight of Bethlehem "   Thomson (Novello)

Resurrection

Children: " Song for Easter "   Eichhorn (Gray)
Adult: " Love Is Come Again "   Whipple (Gray)

Ascension

Combined: " Unfold, Ye Portals "   Gounod (G. Schirmer)

THANKSGIVING FOR OUR FREEDOMS

Prologue

Children: " Come, Together Let Us Sing "
     Bach (E. C. Schirmer)

Adult: " Glorious Forever, Our Freedom Giver "
Rachmaninoff (Boston)

Freedom from Want

Children: " A Child's Prayer "   Taylor (Oxford)
Children: " Blessing "   Curran (G. Schirmer)
Adult: " List to the Lark "   Dickinson (Gray)
Adult: " Now Thank We All Our God "
Crueger-Mueller (G. Schirmer)

Freedom from Fear

Adult: " He Who Would Valiant Be "
Broughton (G. Schirmer)
Adult: " The Lord Is My Shepherd "   Mueller (C. Fischer)

Freedom of Speech

An excerpt was read from a Supreme Court decision by
Justice Louis Brandeis, found in *The United Nations Fight
for the Four Freedoms,* Office of War Information.

Freedom of Worship

Jewish Worship
Adult: " The Shofar Is Sounded "   Dickinson (Gray)
Adult: " Our Father, Our King "   Norden (Birchard)

Roman Catholic Worship
Adult: " O Holy Father '   Palestrina (E. C. Schirmer)
Adult: " Let Hearts Awaken "   Clokey (Gray)
    (Based on an ancient plain song melody)

Eastern Orthodox Worship
Adult: " Come and Let Us Return "   Kalinnikov (J. Fischer)
Adult: " Lo, a Voice to Heaven Sounding "
Bortiansky (E. C. Schirmer)

Protestant Worship
Combined: " Worship "   Shaw (Novello)

" SAINTS, APOSTLES, PROPHETS, MARTYRS, ANSWER "
(Biblical — " Saints, Apostles," etc.)

Theme Hymn — " Art Thou Weary, Art Thou Languid? "

Neale

(Sung antiphonally by soloist and choirs)

Moses

Children: " The Ten Commandments "   Pfautsch (Birchard)

Job

Adult: Selections from the Cantata *Job*   Bitgood (Gray)

David

Children: " The Lord Is My Light "   Protheroe (FitzSimons)

Amos

Adult: " Seek Him That Maketh the Seven Stars "

Rogers (Ditson)

Mary

Adult: " Mary's Response "   Christiansen (Augsburg)

Paul

Combined: " Singing with Grace in Your Hearts "

Mueller (C. Fischer)

" SAINTS, APOSTLES, PROPHETS, MARTYRS, ANSWER "
(Post-Biblical — " Saints, Apostles," etc.)

Theme Hymn — " Art Thou Weary, Art Thou Languid? "

Neale

(Sung antiphonally by soloist and choirs)

Saint Patrick (389?–461?)

Combined: " I Sing as I Arise "   Clokey (Concordia)

Saint Francis (1182–1226)

Children: Hymn — " All Creatures of Our God and King "
St. Francis

Martin Luther (1483–1546)

Adult: " Sanctus "   Dickinson (Gray)

John Bunyan (1628–1688)

Adult: " He Who Would Valiant Be "   Cain (Flammer)

Charles Wesley (1707–1788)

Combined: " Rejoice, the Lord Is King "   Pfohl (Flammer)

Albert Schweitzer (1875–   )

Combined: " He Comes to Us as One Unknown "
Marshall (C. Fischer)

THE DOXOLOGY

" Praise God from whom all blessings flow; "
Combined: " Come Together Let Us Sing "
Bach (E. C. Schirmer)
Children: " All Things "   Lewis (Birchard)
" Praise Him, all creatures here below; "
Combined: " Let All Things Now Living "
Davis (E. C. Schirmer)
" Praise Him above, ye heavenly host: "
Adult: " List the Cherubic Hosts "   Gaul (G. Schirmer)
" Praise Father,"
Children: " Praise Ye the Father "   Gounod-Holler (Gray)
" Son,"
Adult: " Carol of the Little King "   Caldwell (Gray)
" and Holy Ghost."
Adult: " Come Thou, Holy Spirit "
Tschesnokoff-Tkach (Kjos)
Combined: " O that Men Would Praise the Lord "
Thiman (Novello)
(This anthem climaxes with " Old Hundredth ")

SEASONAL MUSICAL SERVICES
OF WORSHIP

The Immortal Story of Holy Week

(The titles are suggested in the book *The Easter Story,*
by Felix R. McKnight, published by Henry Holt & Co.,
Inc., 1953. The story of each day as told in the book may be
read before each portion of the service.)

Palm Sunday — Day of Triumph

Combined: " Hosanna "   Bitgood (Gray)

Monday — Day of Authority

Children: " Brother James' Air "   Jacob (Oxford)

Tuesday — Day of Controversy

Children: " Because the Sky Is Very Blue "
                                   Curry (Westminster)

Wednesday — Day of Retirement

Adult: " Christ Went Up Into the Hills Alone "
                                   Bitgood (Westminster)

Thursday — Day of Fellowship

Hymn — " Blest Be the Tie That Binds "   Fawcett

Friday — Day of Suffering

Children: " The Knight of Bethlehem "   Thomson (Novello)

Saturday — Day of Sorrow

Adult: " O Lamb of God "   Howard (Westminster)

Easter — Day of Resurrection

Children: " Alleluia "   Mozart (Flammer)
Combined: " One Early Easter Morning "   Marryott (Ditson)

THE CHRISTMAS CAROL SERVICES

A logical, practical, and interesting outline for Christmas carol services is to have the moods, events, and persons of the Nativity story represented by carols and appropriate Scriptures.

One form of this may be:

The Heavenly Hosts

Adult: " As It Fell Upon a Night "   Davis (Galaxy)
Combined: " When the Sun Had Sunk "
                                    Knight (G. Schirmer)

The Shepherds

Adult: " Shepherds' Christmas Song "   Dickinson (Gray)
Adult: " Sleeps Judea Fair "   MacKinnon (Gray)
Children: " Carol of the Sheep Bells "   Kountz (Galaxy)

The Manger

Children: " Jesus, Jesus, Rest Your Head "
                                    Niles (G. Schirmer)
Adult: " Carol of the Questioning Child "
                                    Kountz (G. Schirmer)

The Mother and Babe

Children: " Sweet Marie and Her Baby "   Niles (G. Schirmer)
Adult: " Sleeping the Christ Child Lay "   Hall (Gray)

The Star

Children: " Now Every Child That Dwells on Earth "
                                                Farjeon (Oxford)
Adult: " Behold That Star "   Burleigh (Ricordi)

The Wise Men

Adult: " Through the Dark the Dreamers Came "
                                                Daniels (Schmidt)

The Mystery of Christmas

Adult: " What a Wonder "   Dickinson (Gray)
Adult: " I Wonder as I Wander "   Niles (G. Schirmer)

Christmas Again

Adult: " Lullaby on Christmas Eve "
                                        Christiansen (Augsburg)
Combined: " Bethlehem " (a medley)   Goldsworthy (Gray)

An outline that is slightly different may be:

'Tis Christmas on the Hillside

Adult: " Hark, Now, O Shepherd "   Luvaas (Birchard)
Combined: " While Shepherds Watched "
                                                Dickinson (Gray)

'Tis Christmas in the Village

Children: " The Birthday of a King "
                                        Neidlinger (G. Schirmer)
Adult: " The Little Town "   Black (Flammer)
Adult: " Still Grows the Evening "   Dickinson (Gray)

'Tis Christmas at the Inn

Adult: " The Inn at Bethlehem "   Dickinson (Gray)

'Tis Christmas in the Stable

Children: " A Child's Wish at Christmas "   Brown (Boston)
Combined: " The Friendly Beasts "   Dickinson (Gray)

'Tis Christmas in Our Hearts

Children: " God Bless the Little Things "   Hatch (Flammer)
Combined: " O Holy Night "   Adam (Ditson)

Another outline takes the phrases of Phillips Brooks's poem, " Christmas Everywhere."

" Everywhere, everywhere, Christmas to-night!
  Christmas in lands of the fir-tree and pine,"
   Adult: " A Christmas Carol from Lapland "
                                    Dickinson (Gray)
   Adult: " Good King Wenceslas "   Sowerby (Gray)
" Christmas in lands of the palm-tree and vine,"
   Adult: " Christ Came to Bethlehem "   Williams (Gray)
   Adult: " Song of Mary "   Christiansen (Kjos)
" Christmas where snow-peaks stand solemn and white,"
   Children: " Jesous Ahatonhia "   de Brebeuf (G. Schirmer)
" Christmas where cornfields lie sunny and bright,"
   Adult: " Christ, the Lord, Is Born "   Bitgood (Galaxy)
" Christmas where children are hopeful and gay,"
   Children: " How Far Is It to Bethlehem? "   Shaw (Novello)
   Children: " The Flute Carol "   Couper (J. Fischer)
" Christmas where old men are patient and gray,"
   Children: " A Chinese Christmas Carol "   Wiant (Gray)
" Everywhere, everywhere Christmas to-night! "
   Children: (" *Each in his own tongue* ")
         " Stille Nacht! Heilige Nacht! "
         " Un Flambeau, Jeannette, Isabella "
         " Adeste, Fideles, Laeti, Triumphantes "
" For the Christ-child who comes is the Master of all,"
   Combined: " All Were There "   Lynn (Ditson)
" No palace too great and no cottage too small."
   Combined: " Nazareth "   Gounod (C. Fischer)

A Service of Thanksgiving

Thanksgiving for the Seasons

" Blessed be the name of God for ever and ever, . . .
He changes times and seasons." — Dan. 2:20-21.
Children: " A Child's Thanksgiving "   Baynon (Oxford)

Thanksgiving for Our Country

" The land which the Lord your God gives you." — Deut. 27:2.
Adult: " All Praise to God the Eternal "   Gaul (J. Fischer)

Thanksgiving for Temporal Blessings

" Forget not all his benefits." — Ps. 103:2.
Children: " I So Often Wonder "   Jones (C. Fischer)
Children: Hymn — " I Thank You, God, for This Good Day "
Morton

Thanksgiving of the Psalmist

Adult: " Psalm One Hundred and Fifty "   Franck (Ditson)

Thanksgiving of the Pharisee

" I thank thee that I am not like other men." — Luke 18:11.
Solo: " The Publican "   Van de Water (Ditson)

Thanksgiving for Choice

" Choose this day whom you will serve." — Josh. 24:15.
Adult: " The Ways " (as choric speaking and hymn)
Oxenham-Day (*The New Hymnal for American Youth*)

Thanksgiving for Memory

" I thank my God in all my remembrance of you." — Phil. 1:3.
Male Quartet: Hymn — " The Church in the Wildwood "
Pitts

The Supreme Reason for Thanksgiving
" God so loved the world that he gave his only Son."

— John 3:16.

Children: Hymn — " I Am So Glad that Jesus Loves Me "

Ascribed to Oakey

MUSICAL SERVICES
AND SOCIAL PROBLEMS

With the world suffering from international tensions externally and from social and racial unrests internally, persons whose lives are devoted to music, a peaceful art, are apt to feel helpless. Of what use are music and the musician in the face of misunderstanding and mistrust? Much has been written about the morale-building influence of music in the life of a nation; little, concerning the more positive functions of music in times of social restlessness. What can the church musician, or any other, for that matter, do in his restricted field toward bringing about understanding between people?

The conscientious choir director will find that there are times when either by subtle suggestion or by bold declaration he can let his music affirm the universal brotherhood of man. He can show by the nature of the programs he arranges and the music he selects that " humanity is one." The President of the United States, by proclamation, sets aside one week each February as " Brotherhood Week." This gives the alert director an appropriate occasion to present an interfaith choral program, a program of Negro spirituals, or a service of Jewish and Christian music. Another very appropriate time for Jewish music in the Chris-

tian church is the Sunday between Rosh Hashana and
Yom Kippur, usually falling around the first of October.

However, it is not necessary to wait for occasions. The
director who is sensitive to the social and racial injustices
of our generation and is eager to do what he can to correct
them will make opportunities for programs of this nature.
A service of interfaith choral music gives satisfaction in
preparation and presentation. It is timely. There can be
fine contrast in styles of composition, making a well-bal-
anced program. The director may present a program such
as this:

From the Jewish Synagogue

" Sh'ma Yisroel " (sung in Hebrew and English
           Gaul (Galaxy)
" The Twenty-third Psalm " Fromm (Transcontinental)

From the Eastern Orthodox Church

" We Praise Thee "   Schvedoff (Boston)
" God Is with Us "   Kastalsky (J. Fischer)

From the Roman Catholic Church

" Alleluia, Lord God " (sung in Latin or English)
         Palestrina (E. C. Schirmer)
" Let Hearts Awaken " (plain song) Clokey (Gray)

Spiritual Folk Songs

" Our Master Hath a Garden " Clokey (Birchard)
" A Song in Praise of the Lord " Dickinson (Gray)

Negro Spirituals

" Steal Away "   Hall (Rodeheaver)
" Were You There? "   Burleigh (Ricordi)

Protestant Worship

" Now Thank We All Our God "
Crueger-Mueller (G. Schirmer)
" The Lord Bless You "
Lutkin (Summy)

Such a program may be titled " Freedom of Worship."
By eliminating the Jewish portion, it may be used to throw
musical light on the growing trend toward a more friendly
relationship among all the churches that believe in Christ.
Used in this way it may be titled " An Ecumenical Musical Service."

Jews and Christians have much in common. The wise
person will magnify the mutual beliefs and minimize the
differences. We join in the same psalms of praise; we worship the same God.

" Sh'ma Yisroel, Adonoy elohenu Adonoy echod."
" Hear, O Israel: The Lord our God is one Lord."
— Deut. 6:4.

Many portions of the Jewish liturgy are usable in the
Protestant service. The director can find many anthems
based upon Jewish hymns or traditional melodies in the
various publishers' catalogues. Most hymnals contain the
hymn tunes " Rock of Ages " and " Yigdal (Leoni) " or
others based upon ancient Hebrew melodies. Dickinson,
Gaul, Freed, Block, Castlenueovo-Tedusco, Beimal, and
several others have composed organ numbers based on
Jewish music. Thus it may be seen that there is much material available. It is practical to base all the music in a
special Protestant service on the musical expressions of the
synagogue. Your neighboring rabbi, hearing of your program of Jewish music, may ask you to sing it for his people.
This friendly request should not go unheeded. It is a
good experience for all concerned.

In some communities it may be but a flicker, in others a flame, but everywhere to some degree there is a Negro problem. Or is it a white problem? It is time that Christians everywhere set an example and call to the striving factions in Oxenham's challenging words:

> " Join hands, then, brothers of the faith,
>   Whate'er your race may be!
>   Who serves my Father as a son
>   Is surely kin to me." [51]

A service of Negro spirituals will prove both helpful and delightful. If a colored choir or soloist and minister join a white choir, it is that much more effective in accomplishing the interracial harmoniousness desired.

The publishers' catalogues have a liberal supply of well-edited spirituals. Some may not sound effective when used by a white group, but many will be very successful and conducive to worship. The writer does not like spirituals that are " overcomposed " or filled with modern harmonic effects. He prefers the simpler forms as edited by sensitive Negro composers such as Harry Burleigh, R. Nathaniel Dett, Hall Johnson, and others. Some hymnals include spirituals arranged as hymns for congregational singing. There is an ample supply of solos of Negro origin. Effective organ material based upon spirituals is not too abundant, but it may be found (Kemmer's " Prelude on the Negro Spiritual ' Deep River,' " published by G. Schirmer, Inc., for example) . Thus we find there is sufficient material for diversified, well-rounded services of music from the religious utterances of our colored brothers.

It is commonly said that church choirs have two functions: first, to lead the congregation in its musical expressions of praise and prayer; second, to minister to the congregation through the interpretation of sacred choral art. To these let us add another: to help, even though in a small way, in the solving of the social and racial problems of our day.

CHOIR DEDICATION SERVICE

To impress upon the singers and the congregation the responsibilities assumed in choir membership, it has been found helpful to have a service of dedication each fall as the new season's work is undertaken. The material may be simple or elaborate; it may be a part of a morning worship hour or be used in a separate service. Whenever used, it should be carefully prepared by the pastor, minister of music, and choristers; it must be a sincere act of consecration and dedication.

A choir dedication service may well include some or all of the following:

A presentation of the choristers by the minister of music

Scriptural injunctions

A creed for choristers

A hymn stanza of consecration

A litany of dedication

A charge by the minister

A pledge of dedication

A choral prayer

An anthem of dedication

It is suggested that when the choir comes forward during the processional hymn, it form in front of the chancel, facing the minister. The minister of music should go to the lectern to make the presentation of the singers to the pastor and the congregation. Such a presentation may be:

" Music ever has served as a handmaiden of religion. In the Old Testament we find many references to vocal and

instrumental music being employed in the worship of God. New Testament Christianity was introduced by the singing of the angels at the birth of our Savior. The early church expressed its worship in ' psalms and hymns and spiritual songs.' And so, even unto today, followers of the true God have used music to express their prayer and their praise.

" Standing before you are singers who have expressed a willingness to lead in the musical ministry in this church this season. They would dedicate themselves today and be charged with their responsibilities."

Here an officer of the church or the minister may read pertinent Scripture passages, saying:

" Hear the words of the Holy Scriptures which apply to your particular sphere of leadership:

" ' Serve the Lord with gladness!
    Come into his presence with singing! ' [Ps. 100:2.]

" ' Sing to the Lord a new song,
    his praise in the assembly of the faithful! ' [Ps. 149:1.]

" ' Sing the glory of his name;
    give to him glorious praise! ' [Ps. 66:2.]

" ' Let the word of Christ dwell in you richly, as
    you teach and admonish one another in all wisdom,
    and as you sing psalms and hymns and spiritual
    songs with thankfulness in your hearts to God.' [Col. 3:16.] "

The choristers may make a statement of their beliefs in a creed such as either of these:

I believe in God, and in his Son, Jesus Christ, through whom there is salvation and an abundant life for all mankind.

I believe in the Christian church and its message to individuals and to the world.

I believe that God is pleased with the sincere worship of his children, and that in the coming together of his followers for praise and prayer and the study of the Holy Scriptures one may help another to the end that there is eternal value for all.

I believe that music can be a helpful part of worship because by its very nature, its moods, and its associations music appeals to the nobler emotions of man and moves him Godward.

I believe that because he has given me musical ability and the will to serve I can be of use in the choir in bringing his message to a needy brother.

or

Leader: Do you believe in God?

Choristers: We believe in God, the Father Almighty, the Maker of heaven and earth. We believe that God is a Spirit and that they who worship him must worship him in spirit and in truth.

Leader: Do you believe in Jesus Christ?

Choristers: We believe in Jesus Christ, Son of God and Son of Man, our Teacher, Example, and Redeemer. We render unto him love, obedience, and adoration, as our Prophet, Priest, and King.

Leader: Do you believe in the power of sacred song?

Choristers: We believe in the power of sacred song, and we believe that, as singers in the choir, we are joining the long procession of choristers who, through the ages, have sung the praises of God and lifted the heart of man.

Leader: Do you believe in the Christian church?

Choristers: We believe in the Christian church, and we are earnestly determined to exemplify its teachings in every relationship in life. We feel a special sense of responsibility to this church, and we will do our best as its ambassadors in song.

A hymn stanza sung by the choir at this point is appropriate. These are suggestions:

" We'll crowd His gates with thankful songs,
High as the heavens our voices raise;
And earth, with her ten thousand tongues,
Shall fill His courts with sounding praise."
(Tune, " Old Hundredth ")

" Take my voice, and let me sing,
Always, only, for my King," etc.

" Come, we that love the Lord,
And let our joys be known; " etc.

" Blessed Master, I have promised,
Hear my solemn vow," etc.

" O Jesus, I have promised
To serve Thee to the end," etc.

" Be Thou my Vision,
O Lord of my heart," etc.

" Come, Thou Almighty King,
Help us Thy Name to sing," etc.

" Let the words of my mouth . . .
be acceptable," etc. (Ps. 19:14)

This litany of dedication, written by H. Augustine
Smith,[52] has been found to be helpful:

" Leader: To a conduct of life worthy of those who
              stand before others in the public worship of
              God,
" Choristers: WE DEDICATE OURSELVES.
" Leader: To help in the fostering of reverence in the
              house of God, and to the creating of an at-
              mosphere of worship,

" Choristers: WE DEDICATE OURSELVES.

" Leader: To lead the congregation in singing the praises of God, and giving the honor due unto his name,

" Choristers: WE DEDICATE OURSELVES.

" Leader: To fill the hour of worship with song and praise and prayer, and to help as we can in the lifting of the burdens of life from all who enter here,

" Choristers: WE DEDICATE OURSELVES.

" Leader: To lead others by song into the Kingdom of God,

" Choristers: WE DEDICATE OURSELVES.

" Leader: To testify in glad and tuneful lay our gratitude and love to Thee,

" Choristers: WE DEDICATE OURSELVES."

The minister's charge to the singers should be direct and forceful. It is not the time to compliment them or to thank them for their services; it is the time to remind them of the obligations of leadership and to instruct them as to their responsibilities to God and his church. As he, the minister, has been commissioned to preach the gospel, so the singers are being commissioned to sing the gospel. As he has to be faithful in preparing for his responsibilities, so they must be faithful in preparing for theirs. As he has to be above reproach in his public and private life, so must they. Our God expects no less of his singing ministers than he expects of his preaching ministers.

If the charge has been as challenging as it should be, it is a natural step for the singers to want to make a public pledge of dedication. Such a statement may be:

Acknowledging my debt to all who have gone before me

in the pathway of sacred song, and trusting in the help of
the Divine Musician, I pledge:

To carry forward the Christian message in music in this
church this season,

To serve the Lord with gladness,

To sing with grace in my heart to the Lord.

or

I will do my best as a member of this choir to show by my
beauty of singing, dignity of conduct, and loveliness
of character the qualities that make a useful chorister.

A choral prayer can bring the dedication service to a
close. The following stanza written by Dr. Earl Marlatt is
uniquely appropriate:

" Deepen my music, O Lord,
    Strike my heart like a lyre;
Sweep its strings till they throb in a chord
    With all things that aspire.
Tune me with mountains and stars,
    Pulsing farther and higher,
Deepen my music, O Lord,
Deepen my music, O Lord." [53] Amen.

This may be sung to the music by Grace Wilbur Conant
written for the hymn " Temper My Spirit, O Lord," and
found in *The Hymnal for Youth,* published by The Westminster Press.

At this point the singers proceed to the choir loft, where
an anthem in keeping with the spirit of the service should
be sung. The following anthems are suggested as suitable:

Name	*Composer*	*Publisher*
" Grant Me True Cour- age, Lord "	Bach	E. C. Schirmer, Inc.

Name	Composer	Publisher
"Now Let Every Tongue Adore Thee"	Bach	E. C. Schirmer, Inc.
"Lo, a Voice to Heaven Sounding"	Bortniansky	E. C. Schirmer, Inc.
"Beautiful Savior"	Christiansen	Augsburg Publishing House
"A Sword"	Woodman-Dickinson	G. Schirmer, Inc.
"God of All Lovely Sounds"	Dickinson	The H. W. Gray Company, Inc.
"A Chorister's Prayer"	Mueller	Harold Flammer, Inc.
"God of Light"	Mueller	G. Schirmer, Inc.
"Singing with Grace in Your Heart"	Mueller	Carl Fischer, Inc.
"Sing We All Now"	Praetorius	G. Schirmer, Inc.
"Let All the World"	Roberton	G. Schirmer, Inc.
"Praise"	Rowley	Oxford University Press
"With a Voice of Singing"	Shaw	G. Schirmer, Inc.

The material suggested above is primarily suited to adult choristers; however, children can participate in the same service. If it is desired to have a dedication service for the children, a separate service is probably best. The litany, prayer, charge, and music can be suited to their age level and thus be made more helpful to them. Such a service can be meaningful and is recommended.

POSTSCRIPT AND CODA

POSTSCRIPT: TO THE PASTOR

A few years ago a symposium was conducted as the concluding session of a seminar on church music held at Chautauqua, New York. Its title was: " If I Were — " The people participating were representatives of those " concerned with the music of the church." On the panel were a pastor, a choir director, an organist, a singer in a choir, a layman from the pews, a parent of a young chorister, a music committeeman, and a composer of church music. Each one was given time to say what he would do if he were in the other's position. Many penetrating and constructive suggestions were made. The counsel given the minister on this occasion did not furnish a complete picture of the ideal pastor-music department relationship, but it did give some good admonitions.

" If I Were the Pastor — "

" I would look upon the choir director and organist as my colaborers, and I would work closely with them. I would know that, if the service is to be an uplifting experience, each leader must understand the goal of the particular service, each minister to the same end. Thus I would decide on the service theme and sermon subject as far in advance as possible and confer with my musicians upon it. I would assume that they were in a better position than I to know what music was right and proper to use. I would leave to them the selection of all materials and the people to perform them."

"I would endeavor to make it possible for my musical leaders to have some 'in-service training' each season at the expense of the church. I would encourage them to attend summer schools or conferences. I would see that this time was not considered part of their vacation period."

"I would consider the members of the choirs my co-laborers also, and I would try to know at least the adults by name. I would attend rehearsals occasionally to show my interest in their work and to understand their problems. Periodically I would publicly thank the choirs for their musical ministry. This would do two things: it would magnify the service of the choirs in the minds of the congregation, and it would be appreciated by the singers themselves."

"I would suggest that two or three times a year the

choirs be given a large place in the morning service. I would not expect them always to have their musical programs in the evening when I know and they know the attendance would be small. Enlarged morning participation would exalt the musical program in the minds of both the congregation and the singers."

" I would not expect the children's choirs to appear each Sunday, morning or evening, in the hopes of attracting a large congregation. I would realize that in their training there are many more activities than learning a song for public presentation and that I should not look upon the choir as an audience-building medium."

" I would try to enlarge the hymn repertoire of the congregation. I would ask my musicians to help me pick worthy new hymns to be part of the ' people's expression of Christianity.' I would encourage the people to sing the familiar ones intelligently and to sing new ones open-mindedly. As occasions arose, I would use the stories of the hymns to make them live in the minds and hearts of the people. I would not inject my favorite hymn into the service too often."

" I would realize that many hymns and anthems in reality are prayers of thanksgiving, of confession, or of intercession and could well be used as parts of my pastoral prayers. This would have an added value of tying the congregation and choirs closer to the prayers."

" I would be aware that the music could ' make or break ' the service, so I would do everything possible to encourage good music, well rendered. Music and preaching are twin approaches to the soul of man; I would make the best possible use of both."

Dr. J. H. Jowett has been most helpful on the minister-musician relationship. He advises the pastor in this wise in *The Preacher: His Life and Work.*

"Enlist his spirit in your own exalted purpose. Make him realize, by the fellowship of your own deepest desires, that he is a fellow laborer in the salvation of men to the glory of God. Let the music be redeemed from being a human entertainment and let it become a divine revelation. Let it never be an end in itself, but a means of grace, something to be forgotten in the dawning of something grander. Let it never be regarded as an exhibition of human cleverness, but rather as a transmitter of spiritual blessings; never as a terminus, but always as a thoroughfare. Therefore take counsel with your organist. Tell him what you want to do next Sunday. Do not be shy about leading him into the deeper things. Do not keep him in the outer courts; take him into the secret place. Tell him your purpose in reference to each particular hymn, and what influence you hope it will have upon the people. Tell him what you are going to preach about, and lead him into the very central road of your desires. Tell him you are going in quest of the prodigal, or to comfort the mourner, or to rouse the careless, or to encourage the faint. Tell him what part of the vast realm of 'the unsearchable riches' you will seek to unveil to your people, and let his eyes be filled with the glory which is holding yours. Take counsel as to how he can co-operate with you, and let there be two men on the same great errand. . . . Never let an anthem be an 'unchartered libertine,' playing its pranks irrespective of the rest of the service — at the best an interlude, at the worst an intolerable interruption and antagonism — but let the anthem be leagued to the dominant purpose, urging the soul in one direction, and preparing 'the way of the Lord.' A preacher and his organist, profoundly one in the spirit of the Lord Jesus, have inconceivable strength in the ministry of redemption." [54]

Here let us return to the " ships " that I mentioned in the Introduction. The one who is ministering with music and the one who is ministering with preaching both need skilled craftsmanship, trustworthy seamanship, and accurate marksmanship. To these let us add a sympathetic comradeship. Then, trusting in the divine help of the Pilot of our lives, the journey of service will be a thrilling and rewarding adventure.

Coda: To the Minister of Music

One more word, if I may.

There are no prefect situations; there are no churches without problems. The grass may appear to be greener across the corner or across the country, but it is probably an illusion. Right where you are there are people who need the help that inspired music and consecrated leadership can give.

Trusting in the undergirding power of the Good Shepherd who said, " Feed my sheep,"

> hear his call,
>> prepare yourself,
>>> follow him in whole-souled service.

> " In simple trust like theirs who heard,
>> Beside the Syrian sea,
> The gracious calling of the Lord,
> Let us, like them, without a word
>> Rise up and follow Thee." [55] Amen.

NOTES

1. By Edwin Hodder, in *The New Hymnal for American Youth,* edited by H. Augustine Smith, Hymn 70. Fleming H. Revell Co.

2. Helpful musicianship pages have been developed by Mabel Stewart Boyter in *My Musical Game Book.* Carl Fischer, Inc., 1956.

3. *Our First Music,* edited by M. Theresa Armitage, Peter Dykema, Gladys Pitcher, Floy A. Rossman, David Stevens, J. Lilian Vandevere. C. C. Birchard & Company.

4. "How Good and Beautiful It Is," Witmark Choral Library. Copyright, 1932, by M. Witmark & Sons.

5. James Bates, *Voice Culture for Children,* Part I, p. 66. Novello & Co., Ltd., 1907.

6. John J. Dawson, *The Voice of the Boy,* p. 31. Laidlaw & Laidlaw, Ltd., 1919.

7. "Teachers of music in the public and parochial schools have long been perplexed as to the treatment of the changing voice, but many are beginning to appreciate the value of the conserved falsetto, largely through the influence of Mr. John Dawson and Miss Elizabeth Van Fleet Vosseller, the founder of the interdenominational choir school at Flemington, New Jersey." (In *The Art of the Choral Conductor,* by William J. Finn, p. 144. C. C. Birchard & Company, 1939.)

8. A book with many helpful ideas on this subject is *Junior Choirs — More Help and Suggestions,* by Elizabeth Van Fleet Vosseller, p. 13. Democrat Printing Office, Flemington, N. J., 1939.

9. *Ibid.,* p. 44.

10. Herbert Witherspoon, *Thirty-six Lessons in Singing,* Lesson 9, p. 17; Lesson 13, p. 20. Miessner Institute of Music,

Chicago, 1930. Also see Herbert Witherspoon, *Singing,* p. 90. G. Schirmer, Inc., 1925.

[11] W. G. McNaught, "Choral Technique," *Proceedings of the Musical Association,* January 15, 1915.

[12] Noble Cain, *Choral Music and Its Practice.* M. Witmark & Sons, 1932.

[13] "The muscles of what we may term the vocal mechanism of the human body are, for the most part, involuntary muscles. Involuntary muscles are not subject to direct control by the will. Their activities must therefore be induced indirectly through willing an act that will automatically cause them to function." (In *The Living Voice,* by John C. Wilcox, p. 2. Carl Fischer, Inc., 1935.)

[14] *Ibid.,* p. 91.

[15] For further help on these problems consult:
Douglas Stanley, *The Science of Voice.* Carl Fischer, Inc., 1932.
James Terry Lawson, M.D., *Full-throated Ease — A Concise Guide to Easy Singing.* Western Music Co., Ltd., Toronto, Ont.

[16] For a study of this phenomenon from the scientific standpoint see Douglas Stanley, *op. cit.,* p. 93.

[17] W. H. P. Phyfe, *20,000 Words Often Mispronounced,* p. 97. G. P. Putnam's Sons, 1937.

[18] *Ibid.,* p. 97.

[19] For further research in this method, see Arthur Edward Phillips, *Natural Drills in Expression with Selections.* The Newton Co., 1929.

[20] From "Co-operation" by J. Mason Knox, found in *The Best Loved Poems of the American People,* edited by Hazel Felleman. Garden City Books, 1936.

[21] Consult the following books with reference to these points:
F. W. Wodell, *Choir and Chorus Conducting.* Theodore Presser Co., revised, 1931.
Noble Cain, *op. cit.,* p. 110.
Henry Coward, *Choral Technique and Interpretation,* pp. 36-37 (pianissimo and perfect pitch). Novello & Co., Ltd., 1914.

[22] William Ripley Dorr, "The Influence of Pitch Upon In-

tonation," in the now discontinued magazine *The New Music Review and Church Music Review,* published by The H. W. Gray Company, Inc. Reprinted from *The New Music* Review by permission of The H. W. Gray Company, Inc.

23 In a pamphlet issued by Gamble Hinged Music Co., Inc.

24 Sydney H. Nicholson, "Relation of Church Music to Musical Life," *Proceedings of the Musical Association,* February 15, 1921.

25 A book of help in the selection of anthems is *Music for the Protestant Church Choir,* by Dwight Steere. John Knox Press, 1955.

26 The following books will be found valuable in the preparation of choric speaking:

Brown, Helen A., and Heltman, Harry J., editors, *Choral Reading for Worship and Inspiration.* The Westminster Press, 1954.

———, *Choral Readings for Fun and Recreation.* The Westminster Press, 1956.

———, *Choral Readings from the Bible.* The Westminster Press, 1955.

Marjorie Gullan, *The Speech Choirs.* Harper & Brothers, 1937.

Agnes Curran Hamm, *Selections for Choral Speaking.* Expression Co., 1935.

Helen Gertrude Hicks, *The Reading Chorus.* Noble & Noble, Publishers, Inc., 1939.

Robinson and Thurston, *Poetry Arranged for the Speaking Choir.* Expression Co., 1936.

Mona Swann, *An Approach to Choral Speech.* Walter H. Baker Company, 1934.

Cecile de Banke, *The Art of Choral Speaking.* Walter H. Baker Company, 1937.

Material arranged for choric speech will be found in *Anthems for the Junior Choir,* Books 2 and 3, and in *Anthems for the Youth Choir,* Book 1. The Westminster Press.

27 See *Vested String Choir,* edited by Gehrkens, Morrison and Williams. The H. W. Gray Company, Inc. Sixteen pieces for multiple string quartet.

Strings in Service, edited by Hinrichsen. Sole agent, C. F. Peters Corporation.

"Brother James' Air," arranged by Trew. Oxford University Press.

[28] Doris Watson, *The Handbell Choir.* The H. W. Gray Company, Inc., 1957.

Scott Parry, *The History and Art of Handbell Ringing.* Whittemore Associates, Inc., 1957.

[29] Walter S. Swisher, *Music in Worship.* Oliver Ditson Co., Inc., 1929. Out of print.

[30] Among them:

David Eric Berg, *The Music of the Church.* The Caxton Institute, 1927.

Andrew W. Blackwood, *The Fine Art of Public Worship.* Abingdon Press, 1939.

Thomas L. Harris, *Christian Public Worship.* Doubleday & Co., Inc., 1928.

William D. Maxwell, *Concerning Worship.* Oxford University Press, 1949.

G. Edwin Osborn, *Christian Worship — A Service Book.* Christian Board of Education, St. Louis, 1953.

[31] Nicholson, *op. cit.*

[32] Charles Wolcott Merriam, *Church Worship Book.* The Pilgrim Press, 1931.

[33] The organ has not always had such a church-wide acceptance. I found the following amusing paragraph in a little book that carried this imposing title page:

"*The Lawfulness, Excellence and Advantage of Instrumental Musick in the Public Worship of God*

"Address'd to All (particularly the Presbyterians and Baptists) who have hitherto been taught to look upon the use of Instrumental musick in the worship of God as unlawful.

"by a Presbyterian (James Lyon) 1763

"An emminent Divine, within the compass of my Memory, in his discourse on the Subject I am contending for, told his Audience there were but three kinds of Beings, that he knew of, whom God had endow'd with Animal Sensation, who were not charm'd with the Harmony of Musick; and they were the Devil, a Quaker and an Ass: But surely had this Declaimer been sufficiently Master of his Subject or had any acquaintance with the World in our Day, he would have included, at least, two whole Societies of worshipping Christians in his Charge: For though indeed the Presbyterians and Baptists hold psalmody lawful, and an important part of divine Worship, yet certain it is, that the miserable manner in which this part of their worship is droll'd out, seems rather to imitate the Braying Asses, than the divine melody so often recommended in Scripture."

[34] *The Problem of Music in the Church,* Bulletin No. IV. Department of Church and Choral Music, Northwestern University, 1930.

[35] From *Poems of Henry van Dyke.* Copyright, 1911, by Charles Scribner's Sons. Used by permission.

[36] All concerned in any way with hymn presentation would do well to read Peter Christian Lutkin's *Hymn Singing and Hymn Playing,* Bulletin No. III, published by the Department of Church and Choral Music, Northwestern University, 1930; also Chapters VI-X of Charles Boyd's *The Organist and the Choirmaster,* Abingdon Press, 1936.

[37] Grove's *Dictionary of Music and Musicians,* Vol. I, article on "Anthems." The Macmillan Comany, 1954.

[38] Waldo Selden Pratt, *Musical Ministries in the Church,* p. 96. G. Schirmer, Inc., 1923.

[39] For helpful information on the chant, consult:
The Hymnal of the Protestant Episcopal Church. The Church Pension Fund, 1940. See instructions on chanting.
Winfred Douglas, *Church Music in History and Practice.* Charles Scribner's Sons, 1940. Many references.
Charles L. Etherington, *The Organist and Choirmaster.* The Macmillan Company, 1952.
A. Hastings Kelk, *The Singing of the Psalms and Canticles to Anglican Chants,* Shorter Papers No. 6. Church Music Society, London, 1925.

[40] For good material see:
Service Music for the Adult Choir, edited by W. Lawrence Curry. The Westminster Press, 1956.

Anthems for the Mixed Choir. Responses. The Westminster Press.

[41] The director will find many usable descants in the following:

Jeanne Boyd, *Descants on Ten Hymns.* H. T. FitzSimons Co.

Russell Carter, *Descants on Favorite Hymns.* Hall & McCreary Co.

Peter Christian Lutkin, *Descants on Familiar Hymns.* H. T. FitzSimons Co., Inc.

H. Augustine Smith, *The New Hymnal for American Youth.* Fleming H. Revell Co.

Donald D. Kettring, *Familiar Hymns with Descants.* The Westminster Press, 1956.

[42] In a paper read before the Musical Association, February 15, 1921, entitled "Relation of Church Music to Musical Life."

[43] In *Church Music in History and Practice,* by Canon Winfred Douglas, p. 259.

[44] In *The Congregation's Part in the Office of Music Worship,* Bulletin No. VIII, published by Department of Church and Choral Music, Northwestern University, 1934.

[45] Louis F. Benson, *The Best Church Hymns.* The Westminster Press.

[46] The following books will be found helpful:

Robert Guy McCutchan, *Our Hymnody, A Manual of The Methodist Hymnal.* Abingdon Press, 1937.

Albert Edward Bailey, *The Gospel in Hymns.* Charles Scribner's Sons, 1950.

William Chalmers Covert and Calvin Weiss Laufer, *Handbook to The Hymnal* (a manual of the Presbyterian *Hymnal,* edition, 1933). Presbyterian Board of Christian Education, 1935.

Armin Haeussler, *The Story of Our Hymns.* Eden Publishing House, 1952.

H. Augustine Smith, *Lyric Religion.* Fleming H. Revell Co., 1931.

[47] Douglas, *op. cit.,* p. 21: "One of the Oxrhynchus papyri (Part 15, No. 1786) contains parts of a Christian hymn, ending with a Doxology . . . Father, Son, and Holy Spirit."

[48] Smith, *op. cit.*, p. 112.
[49] Two of them are regularly found in present-day hymnals: "Awake, My Soul, and with the Sun," and "All Praise to Thee, My God, This Night."
[50] Smith, *op. cit.*, pp. 337-338.
[51] From "In Christ There Is No East or West," by John Oxenham. Used by permission of Erica Oxenham.
[52] "Litany of Dedication," by H. Augustine Smith. Used by permission.
[53] Used by permission of the author.
[54] J. H. Jowett, *The Preacher: His Life and Work*. Harper & Brothers, 1912. Used by permission.
[55] By John G. Whittier. Words by permission of Houghton Mifflin Company.